Political Poetry

Finding the words for real
communication

Christina Walsh

ARCHWAY
PUBLISHING

Archway Publishing books may be ordered through booksellers or by contacting:

Archway Publishing
1663 Liberty Drive
Bloomington, IN 47403
www.archwaypublishing.com
844-669-3957

ISBN: 978-1-6657-4507-9 (sc)
ISBN: 978-1-6657-4508-6 (e)

Library of Congress Control Number: 2023910264

Print information available on the last page.

Archway Publishing rev. date: 06/09/2023

My Poetry is my Mental Health

In verses penned, my solace found,
A therapy, where thoughts abound.
My mind unwound, a healing balm,
In rhyming words, a whispered calm.
Through stanzas formed and metered lines,
I navigate my heart's confines.
My thoughts laid bare, my soul's release,
In poetry, I find my peace.
The words I write, they ebb and flow,
A dance of self, where shadows go.

To parse the truth, to sift the fray,
And understand what I might say.
For meaning's shroud, at times, obscured,
And what I speak, not always heard.
In poetry, I sift and weigh,
To find the truth in disarray.
My therapy, this art so fine,
A sanctuary, a sacred shrine.
To mend the fractures, heal the rifts,
In flowing words, my spirit lifts.
For in these lines, I find my voice,
A chance to grow, to make a choice.
To learn that meaning, oft misplaced,
In poetry, can find its grace.
A balm to soothe the aching heart,
My poetry, a healing art.
In every word, a chance to mend,
In this journey, which I've penned.

Christina Walsh wears many hats as an artist/designer, writer, environmental activist, and sustainability professional, whose words are a powerful call to action and hopefully thought-provoking in the political landscape. Her poetry is a reflection of her deep passion for justice, equality, and environmental sustainability, and her desire to inspire change in the world. With her words, she challenges us to think critically about the world around us, to see the beauty and value in the natural world, and to work together to create a more just and sustainable future.

In this collection of political poetry, Christina Walsh takes us on a journey through the complexities of the human experience, from the struggles of humans to the threats of climate change and environmental degradation. Her words are a testament to the power of art and activism, and a reminder that we all have a role to play in shaping the world around us.

Her words are a reminder that we all have a voice, and that we can make a difference in the world if we choose to stand up and take action.

Www.Walshgalleries.art.   Www.LandRelief.org

*Proceeds of this book will support
victims of the war in Ukraine.*

Contents

Prologue

«Political Poetry» is a collection of political and environmental poetry that explores the complexities of the human experience and the struggle to find the right words to be truly understood.

As poets, we know that finding the right words can be a challenge. We spend hours pouring over our words, searching for just the right phrase or metaphor to capture the essence of our message. We know that the perfect fit can make all the difference, and that our words have the power to inspire, to challenge, and to change.

In the political landscape of today, finding the right words is more important than ever. Our words can be a weapon or a shield, a call to action or a plea for understanding. They can unite us or divide us, inspire hope or sow despair.

Through our poetry, we strive to find the perfect fit - the words that will resonate and help us to be truly understood. We explore the issues that matter most to us, from social justice and environmental sustainability to political corruption and the erosion of democracy.

If these words inspire you, challenge you, and make you think, we hope that they will help you to find your own perfect fit, and to use your poetic voice to make a difference in the world.

Please consider these words,
Their context and intent.
Use them in discussions,
And discord to vent.
But if you put them to music,
You must pay rent.
Just drop me a note,
A check if you will.
To help keep me afloat,
Penning prose daily still.

CHAPTER 1

Politics and Policy

Poetry to navigate the truth of political discourse.

Feminist Foreign Policy

The world is in need of a feminist touch,
A foreign policy that doesn't ignore as such.
The voices of women, marginalized and oppressed,
A new approach, where equality is truly expressed.
A feminist foreign policy, is what we need,
A new perspective, where fairness is the lead.

Where gender is not just an afterthought,
But a central tenet, that cannot be bought.
It's a world where women have a voice,
Where their concerns are not just a choice.
Where policies are based on equality,
And not just on political frivolity.

It's a world where violence is no more,
And human rights are what we stand for.
Where women are free to live and thrive,
And their dignity is what we strive.
A feminist foreign policy, is a path to a new horizon,
Where women and girls are not victims of poison,
or put in prison, and instead, get their rise on.

It's a world where justice reigns supreme,
And equality is not just a dream.
Not if we work together, hand in hand,
To build a world that's truly fair-planned.
Where feminism is not just a policy,
But a way of life, that is truly free.

Book Banning

In lands where liberty is held so dear,
Where minds may wander, free from chains of fear,
A subtle force seeks to hold us down,
Invisible, like shadows, all around.

Book banning, sinister, unseen,
An enemy to thoughts, unclean.
With iron grip, it stifles breath,
Censoring life, it whispers death.

The paper whispers, ink aflame,
Quenched by forces none dare name.
A spark of knowledge snuffed away,
The kindling of a brighter day.

Through corridors of words and thought,
The battles of ideas, hard fought.
In darkest corners, where minds roam,
The seeds of freedom cannot be sown.

They censor dreams, they clip the wings,
Of those who'd soar on knowledge's strings.
The bonds of ignorance, they grow,
And with them, ignorance takes hold.

Yet, from the ashes of our thoughts,
A spark of hope, defiant, caught.
In whispered breaths, the stories rise,
No chain or cage can quell their cries.

The war of words, a storm of ink,
A battle for the right to think.
The shadows dance, the fire burns,
Through books, our minds to freedom turn.

For in the pages, tales unfurl,
Of worlds where truth and wisdom swirl.
No power nor force can break the will,
Of those who seek enlightenment still.

We rise, we stand, we break the chains,
In unity, our freedom gains.
For books, the keys to realms unknown,
Are treasures that cannot be overthrown.

In shadows cast by fearful hands,
A tale unfolds, a somber dance,
Where volumes burn and voices mute,
A dismal song, of silence's tribute.

The embers of a thousand tales,
In ashen whispers, freedom pales,
Through every page torn, every word erased,
A testament of thought disgraced.

What come of the minds that shall not wander,
In these barren lands of candor,
Where zealots sow the seeds of dread,
And curiosity lies choked, near dead.

In darkest corners, thoughts may hide,
Forbidden fruits, the worlds inside,
Where dreams take wing on borrowed time,
And reason flees from shadows' crime.

Yet, brave souls dare defy the night,
With quills of truth, and ink of light,
For every book that's bound and banned,
A spark ignites, a firebrand.

In whispers of a secret prose,
The flame of intellect still glows,
And though the battle rages on,
Ideas find ways to sing their song.

For minds unshackled, unconfined,
We seek solace in the words they find,
And rise above the censors' reach,
In realms where freedom's lessons teach.

Truth Is Truth

Between truth and protected lies, we must decide,
For though we have the right to say what we feel,
We must ensure that what we say is real.
For lies and misinformation, can do great harm,
Can spread like wildfire, like a false alarm,
Can damage reputations, and hurt those we love,
Can cause chaos and confusion, like lightning from above.

So as we exercise our first amendment right,
We must remember the importance of truth's light,
For though we have the freedom to say what we will,
We must ensure that what we say, we can fulfill.
We must be responsible, in how we speak,
And ensure that what we say, is not just to wreak,

But grounded in fact, in reason, and in proof,
For that's the balance, that gives our rights their truth.
When we exercise our first amendment right,
With responsibility, with honor, and with might,
We can ensure that the balance is struck,
Between truth and protected lies, and all the muck.

Loyalties

In the land of shifting loyalties, where votes are cast like dice,
A sea of fickle minds converge, with thoughts both sharp and trice.
They speak of orange juice and eggs, the price of life's embrace,
A measure of a leader's worth, in a world that's lost its grace.
For some, the cost of living seems, a yardstick to define,
The value of a president, and the course of life's design.
But life is more than groceries, and politics a game,
A maze of truth and lies entwined, that stirs the fickle flame.
When bird flu struck, it took its toll, and millions fell away,
Yet blame was laid upon the throne, as if a price to pay.
How long to grow ten million strong, and mend the broken chain?
A question lost in rhetoric, as fickle minds complain.

Gasoline, the lifeblood of an ever-moving world,
A price that skyrockets, as the banners are unfurled.
But who's to blame for record gains, as oil tycoons amass?
A complex web of power, as the fickle moment's passed.
Five dollars a gallon now the tipping point, as patience starts to fray,
A nation held in discontent, as prices rise each day.
But do they seek the truth behind, the riddles that they face?
Or do they simply point and blame, in a never-ending race?
For in the hearts of fickle minds, the answers seldom lie,
A world of shifting sands they see, beneath an open sky.
And so the dance continues on, with every passing tide,
As leaders rise and fall, while fickle minds divide.

In a world of shifting colors, where the winds of change do blow,
The fickle heart of mankind sways, like leaves upon the bough.
They cast their votes with fleeting thought, swayed by whims and tides,
Forgetting that the truth, in twists and turns, often hides.
"Orange juice and eggs are dear," they cry, "and so was Trump the best?"
A notion born of shallow thought, and not the truest test.
For bird flu took its toll, and millions of chickens died,
A tragedy in Biden's time, a truth that can't be denied.

When gas prices soar, oil barons fill their pockets deep,
The cost of living rises, as record profits they do reap.
Five dollars at the pump, is the tipping point we dread,
Yet, people's fickleness remains, and truth is left unsaid.
Why do we fail to see the lies, that riddles often bear?
Are we so swayed by simple things, that we no longer care?

Pause, slow down! Search for deeper truth, in this uncertain dance,
And seek a higher wisdom, as we navigate this trance.
For though the world is fickle, and the **truth** a fleeting flame,
It's in our quest for clarity, that we find our **noble** aim.
In recognizing falsehoods, and the riddles that they weave,
We'll find a path to **understanding**, and the truth that lies beneath.

Vote as if your life depends on it.

Voting is more than just a right,
It's a duty we must not take light.
For if we choose to turn a blind eye,
We let injustice and suffering multiply.

Think of your brother who's gay,
Denied rights and freedoms every day.
Your sister who's missing, her voice unheard,
Her fate unknown, her justice deferred.

Your house on fire or floating down a swelled river,
The world in chaos, nature's beauty withered.
Your parents in need of medical care,
Fighting for their lives, the system unfair.

Your child gasping for air from asthma,
A victim of pollution, an environmental disaster.
Or someone you know, a victim of gun violence,
Their life taken, their loved ones left in silence.

Your best friend, a survivor of assault,
Their trauma and pain, society's fault.
These are the issues that we face,
The consequences of our choices, the human race.

So when you enter that voting booth,
Remember those who need your truth.
Your voice matters, your actions count,
Let your vote be a beacon of hope, a light that can't be drowned.

For if we all choose to stand and fight,
We can make the world a little more bright.
And maybe, just maybe, we can make a change,
For a future that's just, equal and free of pain.

When you go to vote, remember these things,
As if your brother is gay and the joy he brings,
As if your sister is missing, her voice unheard,
As if your house is on fire, and cannot be deterred.
As if your parents are sick and need medical aid,
As if your child can't breathe from the air that's frayed,
As if gun violence has struck someone you know,
As if your best friend has endured a terrible blow.

Your vote is more than just a simple choice,
It's a chance to give someone else a voice,
To fight for justice, and equality too,
To make a difference for me and for you.
So when you go to the polls, remember these names,
And vote with compassion, and not for personal gains,
For the sake of your brother, your sister, your friend,
For a better world, where we all can transcend.

Inequality

In a world of inequality and strife,
Where the female voice is silenced in life,
It's time to open our eyes and see,
That gender equality is what we need to be free.

No longer should we view women as objects,
To be conquered and used for our projects,
But as human beings with unique qualities,
Who deserve the same opportunities.

We must learn to listen and understand,
The strength and wisdom of the female hand,
For women have so much to offer this world,
And their contributions should be unfurled.

Can't we break free from outdated beliefs?
They limit our potential and cause so much grief,
And instead embrace the diversity,
That each unique individuality brings to humanity.

For when we learn to see each other as equals,
We can build a world where all people can excel,
And where gender is no longer a barrier,
To achieving our dreams and making them real.

Can we finally stand together, hand in hand,
And work towards a future that is truly grand,
Where gender equality is the norm,
And all are treated with respect and adorned.

Women's Rights

In a land where freedom's call resounds,
A bitter battle, fierce, unbounds.
The fall of Roe, a turning tide,
A shift in rights, a great divide.
Medication's touch, a choice to hold,
A lifeline for the scared, the bold.
For ninety percent, it serves their need,
In first trimester's fragile seed.
And yet, the cries of rhetoric swell,
Of full-term tales, they falsely tell.
A twisting of the truth's intent,
A narrative that's far from bent.
The lives of women, held in sway,
By those who'd seek to take away,
The right to choose, the right to be,
The masters of their destiny.
No woman should be forced to bear,
A child she cannot love or care.
Reduced to naught but birthing vessels,
In a world where freedom wrestles.
The fight goes on, the hearts aflame,
For every voice, a story claimed.
A chorus rising, fierce and strong,
In unity, they all belong.
To shatter myths, and right the wrong,
To stand as one, a sister throng.
For every woman's life at stake,
A call to arms, a change to make.
And so we rise, against the tide,
To honor those who've fought and cried.
With love and courage, we'll persevere,
And in the end, the truth we'll steer.

City of Angels

Amidst the palm trees and the neon lights,
Where snow and surf come together in embrace,
The City of Angels dazzles in its might,
A place of wonder, beauty, and grace.

The ocean breeze caresses the shore,
As snow-capped mountains loom in the distance,
The warmth of the sun, a welcoming allure,
The chill of the air, a thrilling existence.

In this metropolis of dreams and fame,
The contrasts blend to create a mood,
A sense of peace, a comforting flame,
In this city that's never quiet or subdued.

In the City of Angels, 'neath the sun's warm embrace,
A paradox lingers, a shadow we face,
Where beauty and sorrow walk hand in hand,
A question persists, etched into the sand.

Homelessness thrives in these sun-kissed streets,
While food deserts spread, and despair completes,
The contrast so stark, as we seek to find,
The angelic soul of a city maligned.

Amidst the palm trees, and the bright azure skies,
The heartache of many, through silence, it cries,
How can we be angels, when so many fall,
To the cruel whims of fate, a somber call?

Yet hope, ever resilient, begins to rise,
In the faces of those who dare to surmise,
A city united, a community bound,
To uplift the fallen, and to heal the unsound.

With compassion as our beacon, we take a stand,
Reaching out with open hearts and helping hands,
To feed the hungry, and to shelter the lost,
In pursuit of a dream, no matter the cost.

We build bridges and gardens, we sow seeds of change,
From food deserts, new oases arrange,
In every gesture, big or small, we create,
A vision of angels, that we cultivate.

For in each act of kindness, a spark ignites,
A flame that dances in the dark of the nights,
And as the fire spreads, the city will learn,
The meaning of angels, as hope takes its turn.

In the City of Angels, we'll find our way,
Through love and compassion, we'll seize the day,
And with hearts united, we'll forge a new tale,
In the City of Angels, where kindness prevails.

AUTHOR'S NOTE

My thoughts on elected officials who refuse to defend the constitution or suggest a national divorce: Elected officials take an oath to uphold the Constitution of the United States, which is the foundation of our government and society. If these officials refuse to do so, it is a violation of the trust placed in them by the citizens who elected them and a threat to the very principles upon which our nation was founded. For this reason, elected officials who refuse to protect the Constitution should be removed from office.

The Constitution is not just a piece of paper; it is a living document that reflects our values and guides our actions as a nation. It establishes the basic framework of our government, protects our fundamental rights, and ensures that power is distributed among the branches of government to prevent abuses of authority. It is the duty of elected officials to protect this document, even when doing so may be difficult or unpopular.

When elected officials refuse to protect the Constitution, they undermine the very principles upon which our democracy is based. They may act out of personal ambition, political expediency, or a misguided sense of loyalty to a particular group or ideology. Whatever their motivations, their actions have serious consequences. They may support policies that violate the Constitution, ignore the rule of law, or abuse their power to silence dissent. All of these actions weaken our democracy and erode the trust that citizens have in their government.

Removing elected officials who refuse to protect the Constitution is not an easy decision, but it is necessary to preserve our democracy. When officials violate their oath of office, they betray the trust of the people who elected them and endanger the very foundations of our society. If we allow such behavior to continue unchecked, we risk losing the freedoms and rights that we hold dear.

Removing officials who refuse to protect the Constitution is also consistent with our values as a nation. We are a country that believes in the rule of law, democracy, and individual rights. When officials violate these principles, they undermine the very values that define us as a nation. By removing them from office, we send a clear message that these principles are non-negotiable and that our democracy is worth defending. Don't betray the people's trust.

Some may argue that removing officials who refuse to protect the Constitution is undemocratic or a violation of their rights. However, this is not the case. Elected officials are accountable to the people who elected them, and they have a duty to uphold the Constitution. If they fail to do so, they can be removed from office through legal means, such as impeachment or recall. This is not an infringement on their rights; it is a necessary check on their power.

Healing Health Care

In the land of stars and stripes,
A truth we face, a bitter blight.
A health care system torn apart,
By profit's thirst, a cold, dark heart.
Pediatric wards, they fade away,
No funds to keep, no funds to stay.
For hearts and hips, a higher price,
And children's needs, they sacrifice.
If only they could cast a vote,
These little ones, a voice devote.
Their futures bright, their lives to hold,
A tale of dreams, yet to unfold.
In pregnant mothers, lives at stake,
A truth we face, a heart to break.
On par with lands, where rights are few,
Exceptionalism's veil, askew.
A system flawed, we must confess,
A quest for profit, breeds distress.
Where boner pills and wealth take charge,
And cancer's cure, remains at large.
No longer can we stand aside,
While children's needs are brushed aside.
A change we need, a call to arms,
For care and love, a fight to charm.
In unity, we raise our voice,
For health and life, a conscious choice.
To heal, to mend, to nurture, grow,
For all, not just the ones we know.
Let profit's grip be loosened, torn,
A new day dawn, a world reborn.
For in our hearts, we know it's true,
Exceptionalism starts with you.

For in the land of the stars and stripes,
A tale unfolds, a glaring gripe.
The health care system, flawed, unfair,
Profits placed o'er children's care.
Pediatric units close their doors,
As heart bypasses take the floor.
Hip replacements, grown-up pains,
But children's needs, alas, in chains.
If only kids could cast their vote,
And on their future, they could dote.
They'd cry aloud for what they need,
A voice to plead, a call to heed.
The mothers, too, in fragile state,
Their lives at risk, a dire fate.
On par with lands where rights are few,
Exceptionalism's claims, are indeed askew.
How can we shift the paradigm,
And leave the quest for wealth behind?
To focus on the life, the health,
Instead of profits, stealth and stealth.
For pharmaceuticals and fleeting gains,
Cannot compare to cancer's chains.
A world where answers take the lead,
And profits bow to human need.
We must unite, we must demand,
A system just, a caring hand.
To hold our children, mothers dear,
And chase away the looming fear.
No more the profits, nor the greed,
Let's heal the sick, fulfill the need.
In solidarity, we'll stand,
To mend the system, heal the land.

Red and Blue

In a world of colors vibrant, two shades stood tall,
Red and blue, in opposition, a rivalry to enthrall.
From the east to the west, a divide that's been clear,
A century of struggle, in which hope and fear appear.
Red, the color of passion, of fire and blood combined,
Symbol of a revolution, where old and new entwined.
From nineteen seventeen, in Eastern Europe's land,
A beacon of change, that swept across the sand.
For decades it endured, a flag that flew with pride,
The hammer and the sickle, side by side they'd stride.
A union of the workers, the farmers and the state,
A vision of utopia, or a destiny of hate?

The rise of the red curtain, a shadow cast on earth,
Blue, the counterpart, in constant battle for its worth.
Democracy and freedom, with capitalism's embrace,
Two colors locked in struggle, in an endless, timeless race.
But as the early nineties dawned, the red began to fade,
A crumbling of the empire, and the end of an old crusade.
Yet, in the hearts of many, the sentiments still burn,
The memory of a struggle, that history will discern.
Now, red and blue persist, in battles old and new,
The colors may have shifted, but the fight continues through.
For in this dance of power, the lines are often blurred,
The legacy of bloodshed, continues to be heard.

Democracy and Capitalism

Democracy and capitalism, ideals we hold so dear,
But when three men hold more wealth,
than the rest of us, we fear.
How can we have a fairer system,
when inequality runs so deep,
And the gap between the rich and poor,
seems wider than the sea so steep.

When wealth is concentrated,
in the hands of just a few,
It undermines our democracy,
and our ideals of what is true.
For power becomes concentrated,
and the voice of the people fades,
And the rich use their money,
to influence the decisions that are made.

But we must not lose hope,
and we must not lose sight,
Of the power of the people,
and our ability to fight.
For democracy and capitalism,
can work hand in hand,
But only when the wealth is shared,
across this great land.

So demand change,
and demand reform,
To ensure that everyone,
has an equal chance when they're born.
And work to close the gap,
between the rich and poor,
And to ensure that everyone,
has a fair shot to soar.

For democracy and capitalism,
are not mutually exclusive,
But only when we ensure,
that the wealth is not elusive.
We must work to create a system,
that works for everyone,

Where the few don't hold all the power,
then the many have won.
We should come together,
and demand a fairer way,
Where everyone has an equal chance, to live,
work and play.

For when we work together,
and fight for what is right,
We can build a system that works,
and shine a brighter light.

1. The First Amendment of the U.S. Constitution protects the right of individuals to petition the government for a redress of grievances. This includes the right to participate in public regulatory environmental processes related to environmental accidents and cleanup response.

2. The National Environmental Policy Act (NEPA) requires federal agencies to consider the environmental impact of their actions and to provide opportunities for public comment and participation. Therefore, any attempt to limit or prevent public participation in the environmental process would be in violation of NEPA.

3. The Comprehensive Environmental Response, Compensation, and Liability Act (CERCLA) also provides for public participation in the cleanup of hazardous waste sites. Section 117 of CERCLA requires the President to establish a public participation process for the selection of remedies and the cleanup of hazardous waste sites.

4. The Equal Protection Clause of the U.S. Constitution also protects the right of individuals to participate in the environmental process without discrimination based on race, gender, or other factors. Any attempt to limit or prevent public participation on these grounds would be in violation of the Equal Protection Clause.

5. Finally, any attempt to limit or prevent public participation in the environmental process would be contrary to the principles of democracy and the public interest. The public has a right to know about and participate in decisions that affect their health, safety, and welfare, and any attempt to limit this right would be contrary to the principles of transparency and accountability in government.

Blood Quantum Laws

In a land where freedom's cry resounds,
The echoes of a past confound,
A history stained, pain and loss profound,
Blood quantum laws, their real purpose revealed, found.

To measure blood, a scale devised,
Of ancestry, identities prized,
As whispers of forgotten ties,
Inheritances, now scrutinized.

Invisible chains, these rules impose,
A fractioned truth, divisive blows,
To fracture unity, fragment the whole,
A calculated toll on native souls.

The purpose clear, to disarray,
To quell the pride of ancient ways,
To undermine, to disengage,
A sordid tactic, power's play.

Yet deep within, the spirit thrives,
The heartbeat of ancestral ties,
A tapestry, in colors bright,
Defiant in oppressive night.

For blood, it courses, tells a tale,
Of histories rich, of dreams unveiled,
Of roots that run through time and space,
A legacy, no law can chase.

In recognition of the pain,
The blood quantum laws ingrained,
We strive to heal, to understand,
To unify the fractured land.

The purpose served, now to dismantle,
To light the dark with freedom's candle,
To honor those whose blood still flows,
In harmony, a future grows.

Border Dispute

To call a war a "border dispute,"
Is to cloak it in a veil of muted mute.
It lessens the gravity of the situation,
And leads to dangerous misinterpretation.

The unprovoked war on Ukraine,
Is not a simple dispute, or just a game.
It's a conflict of power and might,
A fight for freedom, a struggle for light.

To minimize it as a mere border brawl,
Is to ignore the forces that do enthrall.
The politics, the aggression, the fear,
That drives this conflict, oh so near.

It undermines the urgency of the matter,
And downplays the role of the attacker.
It's a dangerous way to mislead,
And it's not what the people ever need.

For this war is not just a border dispute,
It's a matter of life, a critical pursuit.
It's a call to action, to protect and defend,
To stand up for what's right, and make amends.

Do not be misled by those who seek,
To hide the truth and make us weak.
See this war for what it is,
War isn't free, peace is.

From Within

In a world where shadows loom, darkness takes its hold,
The enemy we face within, so bitter and so cold.
Domestic terror, fueled by hate, it permeates the air,
As whispers of division, in every corner, we must bear.

A twisted game of politics, where tropes of hate emerge,
A sweet-spot sought in ignorance, as darkness starts to surge.
Anti-Semitic, racist cries, the echoes of despair,
The quest for power tainting minds, a cost we shouldn't bear.

"How low can you go?" we ask, as decency slips away,
A dangerous game, a dance with fire, in these turbulent days.
Appealing to the lowest thoughts, a strategy unwise,
For in the shadows of their words, the truest danger lies.

But still we stand, our hearts aflame, with love to overcome,
For every twisted narrative, a battle to be won.
We rise against the hate that seeks to tear our world apart,
A chorus of united strength, in every beating heart.

No more shall we let darkness win, nor sink into despair,
For in our unity, we find the power to repair.
The enemy may come from within, but so too does the light,
In the face of hate and terror, we stand steadfast and fight.

Stand up and rise above the fray, and seek a brighter day,
For in our hearts, we know the truth: love will find its way.
We reject the tropes that bind us down, in darkness we won't dwell,
Together we'll create a world, where peace and love excel.

Nuclear Blackmail

In shadows cast by Putin's hand,
A game unfolds upon the land,
A dance of power, a chilling call,
As tensions rise and nations fall.

In Belarus, the pawns are placed,
Atomic weapons, futures faced,
Ukraine cries out to the world,
As banners of discord unfurl.

The Kremlin's grip, a hostage held,
Belarus, a pawn compelled,
To host the fires of Moscow's rage,
In this dark and bitter age.

The West responds with aid and arms,
A desperate bid to quell the harms,
While Putin claims to follow suit,
In shadows cast by hollow truth.

The U.N. called, a plea for peace,
To counter threats that never cease,
As nations gather, watch and wait,
The future hangs, a fragile state.

For in this dance of war and dread,
The lines are blurred, the truth misled,
A world united must resist,
The creeping darkness and its twist.

If we stand as one and fight,
Against the shadows of the night,
We'll seek the light of peace and grace,
In this cold and bitter race.

For only when we join our hands,
And stand against the dark demands,
Can hope emerge, a world reborn,
In unity, a brighter dawn.

Woke

"Woke" once a word of pride,
A term of strength and social stride.
It spoke of awareness, of being woke,
To the injustices, the world's smoke.

But over time, it took on new meaning,
An irony, a label of demeaning.
It became a pejorative, a tool of scorn,
Used to mock and belittle, to deplore.

As politics turned, so did the word,
And "woke" became a term that was absurd.
A symbol of the cultural divide,
A way to dismiss, a way to deride.

But we must not forget where it's rooted,
And the message that it once imputed.
Leaving us angry and overwhelmed,
the word now diluted.

But let us not forget the power it held,
The courage, the strength, the passion compelled.
For those who fight for justice, it remains true,
"woke" is still a call to arms, for me and for you.

Yes we can reclaim its meaning, and its might,
To fight for justice, to shine a light.
For in these troubled times, it's needed more than ever,
To break down the barriers, and bridge the divides forever.

This is not just a label or a snide remark,
But a call to action, to ignite the spark.
For "woke" is not just a word,
But a message that needs to be heard.

To fight for justice, to seek to understand,
To walk in others' shoes, to take a stand.
We claim the word back, reclaimed anew,
And give it the meaning it's always been due.
For "woke" is not just a term of divide,
But a message of hope, of change, and of stride.

AUTHOR'S NOTE

The word "woke" has a complex history and has taken on different meanings over time. Originally, it was used as a slang term to describe being aware of systemic racism and social injustices. This meaning emphasized the need to be aware of and actively combat oppression.

However, in recent years, the word has been appropriated and co-opted by various groups, including Republicans, to criticize and caricature liberals and progressives who prioritize issues related to social justice. In this context, "woke" has become a pejorative term used to mock those who advocate for equality and social change, suggesting that they are overly politically correct and out of touch with reality.

The use of "woke" by Republicans to describe liberals demonstrates a deliberate attempt to misrepresent and discredit progressive ideas and values. It serves as a way to dismiss legitimate concerns about systemic oppression and portray those who advocate for social justice as irrational or misguided.

In this way, the use of "woke" has become a symbol of the cultural divide between those who prioritize social justice and those who prioritize conservative values. The appropriation of this term reflects a broader trend of cultural and linguistic appropriation, where marginalized communities' language and experiences are co-opted and stripped of their original meaning.

The word "woke" has undergone a significant transformation over time, from a term used to describe social awareness and activism to a pejorative label used to discredit progressive values. That does not erase it's original meaning. The difference between its cultural roots and its current use highlights the challenges of navigating language and cultural appropriation and the importance of understanding the context and history of words and phrases and emphasizes the deliberate attempt to dismiss that they are making.

If You Don't Stand for Something

In a world that spins with changing tides,
Where truth and falsehood oft collide,
A steadfast heart, a solid core,
These are the things worth fighting for.
When shifting sands beneath us lie,
And whispered winds tempt us to fly,
It's then we find, deep in our soul,
The principles that make us once again whole.
For if we waver, lost and weak,
Swayed by every voice that speaks,
We'll stumble, fall, and lose our way,
In the noise of life's rough play.
So stand for something, pure and true,
A beacon shining through and through.
Hold fast to values that won't bend,
With roots that anchor, hearts that mend.
Be the rock amidst the storm,
A steady presence, calm and warm.
For when we know what we believe,
We gain the strength to never leave.
If you don't stand for something bold,
You'll fall for anything, untold.
But in your heart, with courage bright,
You'll find the path that leads to light.
And as you walk with head held high,
Your principles held to the sky,
The world will see your inner grace,
And follow in your footsteps' trace.

And for the World

World diplomacy is a delicate art,
A dance between nations, a balancing act of heart.
But in these times of turmoil and strife,
The world worries if America's been brought back to life.

With the globe in disarray, and Russia's war on Ukraine,
The world divided, but entwined like a knotted chain.
Our communications falter, our intentions unclear,
The path ahead uncertain, our worries full of fear.

But we need hope, a steady hand,
That NATO can trust to take a stand.
For unity is our strength, and cooperation our guide,
As we navigate these turbulent seas and changing tides.

We could bridge the divides, and build trust anew,
With mutual respect, and a commitment to do what's true.
We should work together, with open hearts and minds,
To shape a brighter future for all humankind.

For world diplomacy is not a game,
It's about the lives we touch, and the legacies we claim.
We must rise above the rhetoric, and reach for the stars,
And strive to build a better world, one that truly empowers.

In this world of nations, we seek diplomacy,
A way to build bridges, and bring unity.
But as the winds of change blow strong,
The world is divided, our future's long.

America's back, or so they say,
But with Foes around the world, can we truly sway?
Russia's war on Ukraine, a constant fear,
As our intentions falter, and communications disappear.

Diplomacy is the key, a path we must tread,
For peace is the goal, and not bloodshed.
We must find common ground, and build upon it strong,
For our world is in need, of a united song.

Entangled futures bind us all,
With communications that often falter and stall.
The hopes of the world rise and fall,
As we seek a steady hand to answer the call.

CRT

In the halls of learning, where young minds take flight,
A battle rages on, to cast or veil the light.
A history cleansed and polished, stripped of truth and pain,
Denies our children's growth, as shadows still remain.

Critical Race Theory, an idea now attacked,
Its purpose misconstrued, the ultimate side-track.
Of understanding, nuance, and a willingness to see,
The myriad of colors in our tapestry.

When we were young, the lessons we were taught,
Carved deep impressions, in our minds they wrought.
And now we stand, as guardians of the flame,
To guide the future, and teach without shame.

Embrace the real history, the servitude and strife,
The struggles of the past, and the value of each life.
To teach of slavery, sexism, and the racism endured,
For in these painful lessons, a brighter path's secured.

By pretending, we steal from the next generation,
The chance to learn, to heal, and build a stronger nation.
To know the truth, the triumphs and the stains,
To forge a future where true progress reigns.

For only in the light of truth, can shadows flee,
And in the hearts of children, a new world we'll see.
A legacy unblemished, by the weight of past mistakes,
We'll teach them to do better, for humanity's sake.

Standing united, as we shoulder this great task,
To offer truth and wisdom, and in honesty we bask.
It's our responsibility, to teach real history,
So the next generation thrives, in a world of equity.

2024

In the land of stars and stripes,
Where democracy once shone so bright,
There brews a storm of hate and spite,
As politics take on a frightening sight.
In the year of 2024, the stage is set,
With America's future on the line,
And back on stage, the man in the red hat,
Threatening to take the world down a dangerous incline.

Trump is back, and he's not holding back,
With his sights set on the White House once more,
Fanning the flames of cultural wars,
And leaving democracy on the brink of civil war.
Blaming Pence for the chaos of January sixth,
With a straight face and no remorse,
He stokes the fires of division and fear,
Pushing America off a dangerous course.
The world watches on in disbelief,
As America's fate hangs in the balance,
With Trump leading the charge,
Towards a future of hate and violence.
But hope remains in the hearts of many,
Who believe in democracy and its power,
To withstand the winds of hate and tyranny,
And keep America from its darkest hour.

We had better hold onto our hats,
And stand up for what is right,
For the fate of our democracy,
Is up for grabs in this perilous fight.
In 2024, the winds of change blow wild,
A nation held captive to a divisive child.
Political strife, a constant churn,
As democracy's foundations start to burn.

The former President, with a smile and a sneer,
Aims to take back what he believes is his to steer.
His words a weapon, his lies a lure,
As he stokes the flames of fear and impure.
He blames Mike Pence for the chaos of January sixth,
While his supporters scream, his ego they fix.
The rabbit hole of hate, he takes us down,
As his base cheers and the rest of us frown.

It's all up for grabs, peace and democracy cedes,
Cultural wars rage and the real wars bleed.
Huddled are the masses, bracing for the storm,
As the nation we love, starts to transform.
But we must not falter, we must not cower,
We must stand up for what's right, and wield our power.
For democracy is fragile, and freedom is not free,
We must fight to preserve it, for you and for me.

Fox News – Is this Entertainment?

In the realm of broadcast news, a twisted game's afoot,
A tale of greed and folly, at the heart of its pursuit.
Is being deceived something we should muse?
Between truth and lies, I think we must choose.
Fox News and Lindell, an alliance quite bizarre,
For in the quest for profit, they've strayed so very far.

The delusions of a top client, they knew his mind was flawed,
Yet still, they gave him airtime, to the world, his views unthawed.
Their biggest advertiser, a siren call for gain,
With conscience cast aside, they chose to entertain.

Where do we go from here, as truth and lies collide?
In a world of shadows, where can reason reside?
To bring the lost ones back, from rabbit holes so deep,
We must untangle webs of lies, and shattered trust we'll sweep.

For those who dwell in denial, of elections gone awry,
We'll light a beacon, strong and true, to guide them to the sky.
With patience, love, and reason, we'll help them see the light,
And gently lead them homeward, from the depths of endless night.

In this age of misinformation, we must hold our light way up high,
To guide the ones who've wandered far, beneath deception's sky.
Through dialogue and empathy, we'll bridge the great divide,
And in the realm of truth and love, together we'll reside.

The path ahead is arduous, a journey to reclaim,
The hearts and minds of those who've strayed, in this dangerous game.
But with conviction, we'll press forward, to mend the broken bond,
And in our quest for unity, a brighter day will dawn.

Truth

In a land of dreams and shadows, where truth once boldly strayed,
A tale of loss and sorrow, a heavy price was paid.
Fox News, the voice of many, with power to enthrall,
In their great hall of mirrors, had cast a twisted pall.

A web of lies, deceitful threads, Dominion's name besmirched,
A defamation case arose, for truth and justice lurch'd.
Seven hundred million dollars and more, the settlement vast,
To make amends, to right the wrongs, to silence lies at last.

But silence came not willingly, nor did it quickly cease,
For those entwined in falsehood's grasp found solace and release.
No public words of sorrow, no admission of their sin,
The truth they kept in shadows, to protect the world within.

And so the bubble thickened, a refuge for the blind,
Where truth and falsehood mingled, and clarity resigned.
The people, lost and wandering, believed the lies they're fed,
Their minds, once bright and curious, now filled with doubt and dread.

For truth in this great nation, a challenge yet remains,
To pierce the veil of falsehood, to break the stubborn chains.
The path to understanding, a winding road and steep,
But hope, like truth, persists, and from the shadows, it will leap.

Oh, America, dear country, where truth shall find its way,
The battle rages on, as night gives way to day.
In every heart, a flicker, a longing for the light,
For honesty to triumph, to guide us through the night.

If we unite, together, and seek the truth we yearn,
To challenge false perspectives and for wisdom, strive to learn.
Only then, within our grasp, the reign of truth restored,
A brighter future for us all, in unity, moving forward.

This land where truth once reigned supreme,
Another tale unfolds, like shattered dreams.
A network stood with twisted aim,
A beacon of deceit, its only claim.

Fox News, a name both proud and bold,
Whispered lies, as they were told.
The truth, it seemed, a distant foe,
A bitter end, like melting snow.

For Dominion's honor, they did besmirch,
A defamation suit, a legal search.
Their lies uncovered, justice sought,
$787.5 million, the price they bought.

Yet within their bubble, no voice was heard,
Of truth, or guilt, not a single word.
A settlement concealed, a secret kept,
The fox, still sly, as its viewers slept.

The truth, it yearned to pierce the veil,
To break the bonds of the lies they'd hail.
But ignorance, a shroud so thick,
Concealed their eyes, a cruel trick.

In this land, divided by desire,
The truth's a flicker, a dying fire.
And though it struggles, its flame so small,
Hope remains, that it won't fall.

We must stand, and fight the fight,
To chase the darkness, and bring the light.
For truth, a beacon, can yet be found,
In hearts and minds, where lies are bound.

The truth, in time, will once more reign,
And mend the fractures, heal the pain.
For America's future, we must believe,
That truth will rise, and lies, they'll leave.

CHAPTER 2

Nature and Science

Power of Nature

Nature is a wonderland, a symphony of patterns and hues,
An orchestra of fractals, and hues of greens and blues.
Under the mushroom cap, we see a fractal world,
A kaleidoscope of beauty, a vision to behold.
The patterns repeat themselves, in smaller and smaller scales,
A grand tapestry of life, a never-ending tale.
The leaves, the branches, and the twigs,
All speak of the fractal nature of things.

From the grandest mountain to the tiniest grain of sand,
Nature is a fractal masterpiece, grand, so grand.
The ferns, the shells, the snowflakes too,
All speak of the beauty of fractals, and what they can do.
Each pattern unique, each one a work of art,
A testament to the beauty, that's always in our hearts.
For nature speaks to us, in a language we can't ignore,
A fractal language, that opens up each door.

Speculate and marvel at the fractals, and their endless charm,
And appreciate the beauty, that's not just a form.
For nature is a wonderland, a fractal masterpiece,
A symphony of patterns, that seem to never cease.

Spring Equinox

Upon the threshold of the spring equinox,
A subtle shift in time, the Earth unlocks,
The days grow longer, shadows start to wane,
As nature's symphony sings a bright refrain.
A tender breeze whispers through the trees,
Awakening life with a gentle tease,
Buds emerge, vibrant hues unfold,
As winter's grip loosens its icy hold.
The sun ascends higher, a warm embrace,
Kissing the earth with its golden grace,
A harmony of renewal, life unfurls,
As flora and fauna dance in joyous whirls.
The mood of the world, once somber and stark,
Begins to brighten, chasing away the dark,
Hope springs eternal, hearts open wide,
As the season of growth sways side by side.
With each blossoming flower, each new-born leaf,
The days gain in time, in beauty and relief,
The world comes alive, in colors so bold,
As we celebrate the stories untold.
Embracing the shift, the promise of spring,
We revel in life, the joys it will bring,
With the equinox near, our spirits lift high,
As we flourish and thrive, 'neath the boundless sky.

Seahorse in the Coalmine

The seahorse, a creature so fair,
With delicate fins and vibrant flair,
Gliding through the ocean's depth,
A wondrous sight that takes one's breath.

But beyond its grace and charm,
Lies a message that sounds the alarm,
For the seahorse, with its fragile frame,
Is the canary in the coal mine, proclaiming a warning flame.

The oceans are changing, this we know,
And the seahorse is here to show,
How pollution, warming, and acidification,
Are causing havoc to their peaceful habitation.

From shallow reefs to deep blue seas,
The seahorse's plight we must seize,
As they suffer from habitat loss,
And the impact of humanity's careless toss.

We can heed the seahorse's call,
And act now before we lose it all,
For as we save this precious breed,
We also protect the oceans we need.

Preserve our marine ecosystem,
For the seahorse and all that swim,
And in doing so, we'll ensure,
That our oceans remain forever pure.

Chicama

In a land where mountains kiss the skies,
Where ancient echoes whisper and sigh,
Lies Chicama, a gem of the sea,
A sacred wave, forever free.

Upon the Peruvian coast she stands,
Carved by nature's gentle hands,
A single point where surfers chase,
The endless ride, a rhythmic grace.

Protected by law, a treasure untold,
Chicama's story, forever bold,
No structures near, no intrusions found,
A pristine beauty, a love unbound.

Two kilometers of untouched space,
Preserving her form, a natural embrace,
A testament to humanity's respect,
For the world's wonders, we must protect.

She dances and curls with the ocean's might,
A radiant beacon in the moonlit night,
A siren's call, inviting and rare,
An endless journey, on a wave that cares.

Oh, Chicama, wave of lore,
Your spirit free, your essence pure,
In your eternal rhythm we find,
The sacred bond of sea and mankind.

For you remind us, noble swell,
That nature's gifts are here to dwell,
In harmony with our hearts and souls,
A lasting connection, a love that consoles.

The Cowbird

In fields of green and skies of blue,
A cowbird's tale I share with you,
A feathered drifter, oft maligned,
Yet, nature's way, so well designed.
Brown-headed cowbird, cunning, sly,
A brood parasite, you can't deny,
No nest you build nor eggs you tend,
On other birds, you must depend.
In shadows cast by early morn,
You watch the nests, a new life born,
A moment's chance, you seize with stealth,
To lay your egg, secure your wealth.
The host bird, unsuspecting, kind,
A stranger's egg, in nest she finds,
But nurturing heart, she does not shun,
She raises it, as if her own.

Your fledgling grows with strength and grace,
Fed by another's warm embrace,
Yet, in this tale, no villain's cast,
For nature's law, it does not ask.
The cowbird, traveler of the land,
A creature of survival's hand,
You play a part, as all things do,
In nature's dance, her grand debut.
We should learn from your design,
To coexist, adapt, and find,
The beauty in each feathered soul,
Their roles in life, their stories told.

Upon a porch, a mirror lay,
Reflections caught, a curious play,
The cowbird sees an unknown foe,
And all day long, the war does grow.

Fierce battles fought with mirrored twin,
A tireless duel, no end or win,
Intrigued, the cowbird cannot see,
The rival there, just fantasy.
Cowbirds wander, a traveler of the land,
A creature of survival's hand,
You play a part, as all things do,
In nature's dance, her grand debut.
No doubt we can learn from your design,
To coexist, adapt, and find,
The beauty in each feathered soul,
Their roles in life, their stories told.

The Golden Spiral

In the tapestry of existence, the Golden Spiral weaves,
A pattern grand, mysterious, in dimensions it perceives.
Not just in human forms, or crystal lattice beams,
But celestial bodies, and the aqua world it gleams.
From the tiniest of atoms to the grandest cosmic scale,
The Golden Ratio resides, a divine, eternal trail.

A sacred geometry, that holds the key to life,
In flowers and in crystals, it thrives through joy and strife.
In every form, proportion, and in the most bizarre,
The spiral bears our knowledge, stretching near and far.
It builds our homes and bodies, constructs our consciousness,
A language of the universe, a cosmic architect's finesse.
In pyramids and planets, the Golden Ratio abounds,
The solar distances it charts, in harmonious, measured sounds.

A secret code embedded, in our cellular memory,
A testament to beauty, truth, and cosmic synergy.
We love the Golden Spiral, a treasure to behold,
In all dimensions it appears, a story to be told.
The carrier of information, the binder of all things,
A cosmic dance of unity, where creation's essence springs.

A Conversation in the Sun

In a tranquil meadow, where nature converses,
The tree, the clouds, the sky, and grass find purpose.
With the wind as their messenger, they whisper and sigh,
A complex tale of love and struggle, a bond they can't deny.
The tree speaks first, her roots deep and strong,
"I love the sky above, but sometimes feel we don't belong.
The clouds drift by, casting shadows on my face,
Yet without their rain, I'd struggle in this place."
The clouds reply, their voices soft and light,
"We share your sentiments, dear tree, in this eternal fight.
We float above, admiring the grass so lush and green,
But often worry we'll smother it with our moisture screen."
The sky, so vast and boundless, joins in the refrain,
"I embrace you all, my children, in sunshine and in rain.
But I too have my doubts, when storms begin to roar,
Do I cause you pain and strife, is my love forevermore?"
The grass then speaks, its blades quivering with glee,
"I cherish every touch, from the wind to clouds and tree.
Though we may quarrel and face moments of despair,
In the end, our love prevails, a bond beyond compare."
The wind, the gentle mediator, rustles through them all,
"I weave your stories together, for I am nature's call.
Through me, you're intertwined, in both love and strife,
A delicate balance, the essence of our life."

The tree speaks again, her branches held high,
"I reach for the sky, yet it makes me sigh,
I cherish our union, our bond and embrace,
Yet at times, I feel trapped in this very same place."
The clouds reply gently, with a soft, tender hue,
"We too feel the struggle, it's quite sad but true,
We float and we drift, yet are bound to the sky,
A love and a longing, that we can't deny."
The sky then whispers, in a voice so profound,

"I hold all together, in this world all around,
And though I'm connected, to each one of you,
At times I feel distant, and somewhat askew."
The grass interjects, with a humble, low tone,
"I'm spread far and wide, and yet feel alone,
I reach for the sunlight, but cannot compare,
To the heights that you touch, it just seems unfair."
The wind then responds, with a breath of fresh air,
"I move and caress, with a touch that's so rare,
Yet, though I am free, I cannot escape,
The feeling of longing, hangs like a shrouded drape."

And so, the conversation weaves, a tapestry of care,
The tree, the clouds, the sky, the grass, and the wind that binds
them there.
In harmony and discord, their love and struggles blend,
A testament to the beauty of the relationships nature sends.

In a realm where the elements convene,
A conversation unfolds, a scene so serene.
The tree, the clouds, the sky, and the grass,
All joined by the wind, in a spirited mass.

In this meeting of elements, their love and disdain,
A paradox lingers, like sun mixed with rain.
Though bound by their nature, they cherish and yearn,
For the freedom to love, and the space to discern.
In the end, they discover, their connections are grand,
Their love and their struggles, go hand in hand.
For even in discord, they share a sweet song,
In the dance of existence, where they all belong.

Venus Passes Jupiter

As night descends upon the earth below,
The stars come out to put on a show,
And in the sky, two planets dance,
As Venus passes Jupiter in a cosmic trance.

The brightest light, Venus, shines so true,
And Jupiter, the king of the planets, comes into view,
Their paths cross, a rare celestial sight,
As they twirl and swirl in the velvety night.

Two orbs of light, so far yet so near,
They twinkle and shimmer, without any fear,
Of the vast universe they traverse,
A fleeting moment in the grand cosmic verse.

As we look up, we feel so small,
But the beauty above us reminds us all,
That there is wonder in every corner of space,
And that we are but a tiny part of its infinite grace.

When we cherish these celestial delights,
As Venus and Jupiter dance in the heights,
We're reminded that in the grand scheme of things,
We are just fleeting moments, stardust on wings.

Directionless

In the realm of Earth, where the compass points stand,
North, South, East, and West, reaching over the land.
They guide our journey, a path to embrace,
Binding us to the celestial, our cosmic face.
As the seasons shift, with each subtle turn,
The Earth's axis moves, a lesson to learn.
We feel the change, the air grows thin,
The world's rotation, a celestial spin.
To the North, we look to the stars above,
A steadfast guide, Polaris' unyielding love.
A beacon of hope, amidst the vast night,
A constant reminder, in the darkness, there's light.
To the South, the warmth of a sun-filled embrace,
A hemisphere's whisper, a gentler place.
As the Earth tilts, we feel it anew,
A season's promise, life breaking through.
To the East, the dawn, a vibrant rebirth,
The sun's first touch on the awakening Earth.
A new beginning, a chance to align,
With the cosmos above, a connection divine.
To the West, the sunset, an ending so grand,
A symphony of colors, a celestial band.
A gentle reminder, as day turns to night,
To cherish the moments in Earth's fading light.
In the dance of the heavens, the Earth's axis turns,
Uniting us all, as the cosmos churns.
We seek our balance, in the stars up above,
Grounding ourselves, in the wisdom they shove.
Align with the Earth, find your place in the sky,
As the axis spins, embrace the change nigh.
For in the celestial North, South, East, and West,
We find our true bearings, our soul's true bequest.

The Oak Tree and the Sun

In a quiet grove, where the oak tree stands,
She listens closely to the whispers of the lands.
The grass below, so tender and green,
Wishes for sunlight, a dream yet unseen.
With a voice so gentle, like the rustling leaves,
The oak tree speaks, her wisdom she weaves.
"I am happy to share the sunlight, dear friend,
You need only to reach, your desires to amend."
The grass, though timid, listens with care,
To the words of the oak, a truth she lays bare.
"Reach for the sky, like the branches that sway,
For the sunlight is yours, just stretch and display."
With a newfound courage, the grass begins to grow,
Seeking the light that the oak did bestow.
A harmonious dance, they share the sun's grace,
Each playing their part, in nature's embrace.
For the oak is a teacher, a mother and guide,
Her roots running deep, her branches spread wide.
To the grass below, she offers her care,
A lesson in reaching, a moment so rare.
In the dance of the sunlight, the oak and grass sway,
Bound by a love that won't fade away.
For the wisdom of the oak will forever remain,
A testament to sharing, the sun's warm embrace.

Beneath Our Feet

Beneath our feet, there lies a world,
Of teeming life, forever unfurled,
A world of soil, so rich and grand,
A place where life takes root and stands.
From microbes and enzymes, to the complex life of man,
Soil is the foundation, on which all life stands.
It's the source of food, that sustains us each day,
The bedrock of life, in every single way.

Without soil, where would we be,
In a world devoid of biodiversity?
For soil is the birthplace, of every living thing,
The heart and soul, of our earthly swing.
From the tiniest bug, to the towering tree,
Soil is the foundation, that sets them free.
It's the key to life, on this earthly plane,
The reason why we can dance in the rain.

I want to cherish this world below,
For it's the reason why our gardens grow,
The reason why we have food to eat,
And the air we breathe, is clean and sweet.
For soil is life, in its purest form,
A world of wonder, forever reborn,
A world of richness, that sustains us each day,
A world of life, in every single way.

Beneath our feet lies a world so vast,
Of soil and earth, so rich and vast,
A world teeming with life so small,
A world we often don't see at all.
The microbes and enzymes that make it thrive,
The very foundations on which life arrives,
For soil is more than just dirt and mud,
It's the source of life, the very blood.

From the tiniest microbe to the tallest tree,
Soil is the cradle of life, you see,
A complex world, so full of grace,
A world we must cherish and embrace.
For without soil, where would we be,
No food to eat, no air to breathe,
No shelter, no home, no life at all,
No world to explore, no grand ball.

This amazing world of soil,
This world so full of life and toil,
For it's the very source of our being,
A world we must care for, with all our seeing.
From the depths of the earth, to the skies above,
Soil is the foundation of all we love,
A world of wonders, so full of grace,
A world we must protect, in every place.

The Beekeeper

In verdant fields where flowers bloom,
And sunlight dances through the gloom,
A humble beekeeper roams the land,
With gentle touch and caring hand.

From plot to plot, his bees he brings,
Awakening the soil with buzzing wings,
A symphony of life, the air is stirred,
As busy workers hum, unheard.

The quiet open spaces come alive,
As tiny bees from hive to hive,
Embrace their task, so vital, pure,
To pollinate and to endure.

The beekeeper knows their sacred role,
To nourish Earth, to make it whole,
For in their toil, life's bounty thrives,
And on our tables, it arrives.

Fruits and vegetables, rich and bright,
A testament to nature's might,
The beekeeper's care, the bees' sweet song,
Together, they help life prolong.

The trees and flowers, they greet each day,
A world of color, a grand display,
Their blossoms kissed by buzzing grace,
A loving bond, a warm embrace.

The beekeeper feeds us with flowering art,
A steward of life, he plays his part,
For in his hands, our futures lay,
As bees ensure our lives' array.

With gratitude, we now partake,
In nature's gifts, for all to make,
The beekeeper's love, the bees' sweet labor,
A dance of life, for all to savor.

Drought Profiteers

In Arizona's land of desert sun,
A tale of greed and thirst begun,
Where rivers trace the earth's embrace,
The profiteers reach extends its pace.

Upon the ground where cacti dwell,
The Wall Street firms their stories tell,
As farmers' soil turns into gold,
In hands of giants, rights are sold.

They buy the land, they claim the source,
Of life itself, they bend its course,
The Colorado's vital flow,
In drought profiteers' grasp doth go.

The water scarce, the rivers drained,
The desert cries in arid pain,
The people's thirst ignored and tossed,
A price we pay, a beauty lost.

The land, once home to life untamed,
Now shackled by the greed inflamed,
The wildlife suffers, forced to flee,
Their refuge sold for human's spree.

But we the people hold the key,
To fight the greed, the drought to free,
In unity we stand, we plead,
To break the chains of endless greed.

With conscious choice and firm resolve,
We'll turn the tide, the truth absolve,
No more a slave to profit's creed,
We'll save the land, the rivers freed.

As they pillage, they should take heed,
For we shall rise and not concede,
With voices strong, we'll make our stand,
And halt the drought's oppressive hand.

Cosmic Connections

Upon the realm of Venus, bright,
A fiery wonder comes to light.
A tale of sister worlds entwined,
In cosmic dance, their fates aligned.
A volcano's breath, a scorching plume,
In Venus' skies, a fiery bloom.
A distant kin to Earth's own core,
A tale of parallels we'll explore.

What secrets lie within its flame?
What parallels to Earth's own claim?
A kinship shared, a mirrored birth,
Two sisters bound by cosmic girth.
We search for truth, a shared embrace,
The lessons gleaned from Venus' face.

Its fiery heart, a beacon bright,
A testament to nature's might.
The magma's flow, the molten veins,
Infernos' dance, their wild refrains.
A mirror to our own world's strife,
The power of creation's life.
In Venus' fire, a tale untold,
Of how our planets' fates unfold.

A link to forge, a bond to share,
Through cosmic dance, a truth laid bare.
For in the blaze, we seek to find,
A glimpse of Earth's own kindred mind.
A tale of life, of death, of birth,
In fiery hearts of cosmic mirth.
And so, we watch, as Venus glows,
With newfound wonder, knowledge grows.

A bridge across the starry skies,
A tale of sister worlds' demise.

Dragons Beneath

Beneath the earth's surface, a secret world lies,
Where roots turn to dragons, and battles arise,
In the shadows they dwell, fierce and unseen,
A realm of enchantment, where life breathes serene.

These ancient creatures, their forms twist and wind,
As they forge their dominions, the soil they bind,
Their scales of bark, a shield against strife,
In the darkness, they challenge for territory and life.

A symphony of whispers, they hiss and they roar,
Claws of deep roots, they scratch and they bore,
Their breath ignites life, as they exhale in might,
Entangled in combat, in their ceaseless fight.

For the land they defend is more than it seems,
A sanctuary of secrets, a realm of dreams,
Each dragon, a guardian of the world up above,
Their struggles, a testament to the depths of their love.

They vie for the right to nourish the land,
With their blood in the soil, the forests they've planned,
Their battles unseen, as they weave and they sway,
But the strength of the trees betrays the fierce fray.

So when next you walk through a forest so grand,
Pause for a moment, let your thoughts expand,
For beneath your feet, where the dragons reside,
A world of wonder, in the roots of trees, they hide.

Ceiba Tree

In Vieques, proud and tall it stands,
A Ceiba Tree, midst emerald lands.
A witness to the centuries past,
In silent strength, its roots held fast.

A hug bestowed, a sacred tie,
Between a tree and those nearby.
A bond that heals, a bond that mends,
In heart and soul, the spirit blends.

Majestic Ceiba, wise and grand,
With unseen eyes, you watch the land.
A sentinel of time and space,
A living bridge, a warm embrace.

If trees had eyes, what tales they'd share,
Of love and loss, of joy, despair.
The secrets whispered to the breeze,
A chronicle of life's mysteries.

They'd speak of storms that raged and roared,
Of sunny days, and lovers' chords.
Of children's laughter, free and wild,
Of wisdom shared, of hope compiled.

To hug a tree, a gift profound,
A moment's peace, a solace found.
For in that touch, we come to see,
The world's vast web, its tapestry.

So wrap your arms around its girth,
Embrace the heart of Mother Earth.
A hug that mends, a hug that heals,
In Ceiba's arms, our spirits kneel.

And as we hold the tree so tight,
We glimpse the world in dappled light.
A deeper truth, a wisdom gained,
In Ceiba's arms, our souls sustained.

Cassowary's Prehistory

The cassowary, a bird most rare,
With vibrant hues and striking glare,
A remnant of prehistoric days,
With curious traits, it oft amaze.
Three species in the family dwell,
In rainforests where secrets swell.
The Southern, Dwarf, and Northern kind,
Each one, a wonder to unwind.
With towering crest, the casque, it wears,
A helmet for the fights it bears.

Its purpose still remains unknown,
A mystery of nature, grown.
A dinosaur-like gait, it strides,
With razor-sharp claws, it glides.
A deadly kick, it can unleash,
A force of nature, wild and fierce.
This flightless bird, in forests deep,
A solitary life, it keeps.
Its call, a low and rumbling boom,
Resounds beneath the jungle's gloom.
A frugivore, on fruit it thrives,
Dispersing seeds, where life survives.

A keystone species, it sustains,
The balance in its rich domains.
Cassowaries swim with grace and ease,
Across the rivers, through the seas.
Their prowess in the water shines,
An unexpected skill, defines.
These vivid, ancient birds, we find,
Hold secrets that still baffle minds.
A living relic from the past,
May their allure forever last.

The Moon Dressed like Saturn

In the cosmic masquerade, where celestial wonders play,
A night of whimsy beckons, as the moon prepares the way.
Adorned in gown of cloud swirls, and light that ebbs and flows,
She takes the stage as Saturn, in a dance that's grandiose.
The audience of stars looks on, their twinkling eyes aglow,
As the moon transforms before them, in an ethereal tableau.

Her wisps of cloudy rings encircle, a Saturnine embrace,
A veil of pale illusion, with delicate, shifting grace.
The light it bends and shimmers, like ribbons in the sky,
As the moon pirouettes and glides, her elegance soaring high.
A ballet of the heavens, as she mimics Saturn's grace,
A cosmic waltz of beauty, through the vast, celestial space.

And in this fleeting moment, the universe aligns,
A celestial celebration, where the moon and Saturn twine.
The planets gaze in wonder, as the moon takes center stage,
Her borrowed guise of grandeur, a testament to the age.
Soon the night must end, and the moon will shed her cloak,
Returning to her lunar form, as dawn begins to broke.
But in the hearts of those who watched, the memory will burn,
Of the night when moon as Saturn danced, a cosmic tale to learn.

Monarch Love

Amidst the fields of flowers, light as air,
The monarch butterfly takes to the sky,
Undaunted by the miles they must bear,
Their journey a wonder that can't be denied.

One generation rises, then they fade,
Their offspring carry on, without a break,
And in this way, a great migration's made,
A journey that no other can quite make.

But now, the world is changing all too fast,
Climate change and pesticides take their toll,
And though they try, the butterflies can't last,
Against these threats, they struggle to be whole.

The monarch butterfly, is so brave and true,
We must do more to ensure life for you. Join us at Landrelief.org

Perfect Alignment

In the depths of space, a rare sight to see,
Four planets align in perfect symmetry,
Jupiter, the giant, with its swirling storms,
Saturn, with rings, in orbit it forms.
Venus, the brightest, shimmers with light,
Mars, the red planet, shines through the night,

As they align in celestial dance,
Their beauty captures our every glance.
Jupiter, the king, of all the planets,
A massive presence, its size, immense,
Saturn, with its rings, a cosmic jewel,
A breathtaking sight, a cosmic fuel.

Venus, the goddess of love and grace,
A shining star, in the sky's embrace,
Mars, the fiery red, a warrior's might,
Together, they form a stunning sight.
As they align, a cosmic spectacle,
A sight so rare, it's almost mythical,

A reminder of the vastness of space,
And the wonders that it can embrace.
Four planets, in perfect alignment,
A heavenly display, a true refinement,
A reminder of the universe's vastness,
And its endless cosmic dance.

Monet

In the haze of yesteryear's skies,
Where soot and smoke did blend,
A master's eye would realize
A canvas to transcend.

Monet, with strokes so delicate,
Turner, with fiery hue,
Captured light and air innate,
A dreamlike world imbue.

The engines roared, their steam released,
As factories churned away,
Air pollution's grip increased,
In London's skies and Paris' fray.

And yet, the artists saw the chance
To paint in mystic light,
The beauty held within the dance
Of colors soft and bright.

As particles obscured the view,
The edges blurred and bled,
A spectral scene of opal hue,
A canvas vast and spread.

In letters penned to wife so dear,
Monet did once confide,
The smoky shrouds did inspiration steer,
His muse, the hazy tide.

From contamination's grasp emerged
A world of beauty rare,
Where light and shadow intertwined
And danced upon the air.

We cannot forget the bond
Between the dark and light,
For from the depths of murky fog,
May brilliance take its flight.

The Call of Space

The stars above, so vast and bright,
Spark a yearning in us to take flight,
To venture forth beyond this place,
And explore the mysteries of space.

The pull of planets, the call of moons,
A universe waiting for us to zoom,
The wonder and awe of the unknown,
To boldly go where we've never flown.

We dream of ships that can traverse,
The vastness of space, the cosmic universe,
And see the beauty that lies beyond,
To seek out what we've yet to find.

But as we reach for the stars above,
We must remember our earthly love,
To care for the planet we call home,
To ensure its health and safety, we must roam.

For the work of space, the technology we seek,
Can leave a trail of toxins, polluting our peak,
We must be mindful of the impact we make,
And clean up our mess for future's sake.

The yearning for space, the desire to explore,
Must go hand in hand with the need to restore,
The planet we call home, our precious earth,
So that future generations may know their worth.

We can journey to the stars above,
With a mission to cherish our earthly love,
To seek out the answers that we seek,
And clean up the toxins, to keep our planet's peak.

Earthly Sphere

In distant space, beyond our earthly sphere,
A reservoir of water lies in wait,
A vast expanse of liquid, pure and clear,
Beyond all measure, vast and intricate.

Its volume dwarfs the oceans of our world,
A hundred forty trillion times the sum,
Of all the waters, every wave unfurled,
In every sea, in every ocean run.

This cosmic sea, in silence, ebb and flow,
A source of wonder, mystery, and awe,
Its secrets hidden, yet to be made known,
To human eyes, so fragile and so small.

A wondrous reservoir, so vast and grand,
May we one day explore your distant strands.

Center of the Earth

To see into the center of the earth,
Would be a journey of endless worth,
A glimpse into a world so vast,
A world of wonder, must be wildly unsurpassed.
We might see the molten core,
A fiery world, that we'd adore,
A world of lava, heat, and flame,
A world that we'd never be the same.
We might witness the shifting plates,
A tectonic dance, that never abates,
A world in constant motion and change,
A world that's both wild and strange.
We might glimpse the secrets of time,
The layers of earth, a story sublime,
A tale of ages, that we'd learn to read,
A story of life, that we'd come to heed.
We might find life, in the deepest deep,
A world of creatures, that we'd want to keep,
A world of wonder, so full of surprise,
A world that would open up our eyes.
To see into the center of the earth,
Would be a journey of endless worth,

For the Birds

No matter what yesterday was like,
No matter the struggles or the strife,
The birds start the new day with a song,
A melody that echoes all day long.
They sing of hope, they sing of grace,
A message of love, that they embrace,
A song that lifts our hearts up high,
And fills our souls with joy and sigh.
For the birds, each day is a new start,
A chance to live, to love, and to impart,
Their message of hope, to all who hear,
To chase away doubts, and conquer fear.
They sing of the beauty that surrounds,
Of the wonders of life that abounds,
Of the endless possibilities that await,
A message of hope, that they don't debate.
Learning from the birds that sing,
And embrace each new day with a wing,
A chance to start anew, and to be,
The best that we can, for all to see.
For no matter what yesterday was like,
We can always start anew, and take flight,
With hope and love, in our hearts so strong,
And embrace each new day, with a song.

No matter what yesterday brought,
No matter how we may have fought,
The birds start the new day with a song,
A melody so sweet, it can never be wrong.
Their chirps and tweets, a symphony,
A reminder that life is a gift, a mystery,
That every day is a chance to start anew,
To let go of the past, and embrace what's true.
For the birds, there's no yesterday,

No worries or fears, to hold them at bay,
Just the present moment, full of hope,
A chance to fly, and learn to cope.
Here we can learn from the birds of the sky,
And start each day with a joyful sigh,
No matter what yesterday may have brought,
For the future is a canvas, yet to be wrought.
Sing with the birds, and dance with the trees,
Embrace the beauty of life, with childlike glee,
For every day is a gift, a chance to be free,
And the birds' sweet song, a reminder to see.

The Great Horned Owl

The great horned owl, a bird of might,
With wings that spread, and eyes that light,
A creature of the night, so wise,
It watches the world beneath it as it flies.

Its song, a hoot that echoes through the trees,
A sound that carries on the midnight breeze,
A call that speaks of ancient lore,
Of wisdom and knowledge, forevermore.

With feathers soft as snow, and eyes that gleam,
This bird of prey is a formidable team,
A hunter swift, with talons sharp,
It soars through the night with a thunderous heart.

Its beat, a rhythm that shakes the earth,
As it takes to the sky, with power and mirth,
The great horned owl, a creature of flight,
A symbol of wisdom, in the dark of night
We marvel at this bird of might,
And listen as it sings into the night,
For the great horned owl, a wonder to behold,
A creature of beauty, so brave and bold.

The Native Garden

A garden filled with life and light,
Where bees and butterflies take flight,
And hummingbirds dance in the air,
A peaceful place without a care.
The colors bloom in every hue,
A vibrant scene, so fresh and new,
The fragrance fills the summer air,
A tranquil space, beyond compare.
We see and cherish this native land,
And all the creatures that make it grand,
For in their dance, we find our peace,
And in their stillness, all our release.

In the native garden, so full of life
Bees, butterflies, and hummingbirds thrive
Their colors and movements, a dance so bright
In the sun, they shine with such might
The flowers and plants, they sway in the breeze
Their fragrances, carried with such ease
The garden, a symphony of sounds and hues
A place of peace, where nature's beauty soothes.

Cooper's Hawk

A Cooper's hawk, so fierce, so sly
And suddenly, the garden falls silent
As all the creatures hide, quite compliant
A shadow passes by,
A Cooper's hawk, majestic and sly,
The garden falls into silence now,
As all creatures hide and bow.
The hawk perches on a nearby tree,
And watches on, so wild and free,

A part of nature's wondrous dance,
In this garden, so full of chance.
For in this moment, all is still,
As nature's law takes over at will,
And in this balance, we see the truth,
Of life's cycles, from birth to youth.
And yet, as the hawk takes flight and is gone
The garden resumes its peaceful song

The bees, butterflies, and hummingbirds return
And the garden, once again, begins to churn
For in this native garden, so full of life
There is a balance, a beauty, so rife
Where excitement and peace can coexist
And nature's beauty can truly persist.

After the Rain

After the rain, the forest awakens,
With a beauty that cannot be mistaken.
The air is fresh, the leaves are green,
And the flowers and plants, are a sight to be seen.
The pollinators, they emerge from their shelter,
To explore the forest, and seek out new treasure.

The bees, the butterflies, the hummingbirds too,
Are the guardians of the land, and the keepers of the true.
For after the rain, the forest comes alive,
With the buzzing of the bees, and the flutter of the butterflies.
The flowers and plants, they thrive and bloom,
And the pollinators, they dance and swoon.

The beauty of the forest, after the rain,
Is a reminder, of the wonders that remain.
And the pollinators, they are the key,
To the balance of life, that we so desperately need.
Marvel, pause, and cherish the beauty of the forest,
And work to protect it, with all our best.
For the pollinators, they are the keepers of the land,
And the beauty of the forest, is in their gentle hand.

The Cliffs of the Peregrine

Upon the cliffs, the peregrine makes its home,
A fierce predator, with wings that roam,
A master of the skies, it soars and dives,
To hunt and gather, and keep its young alive.

But danger lurks, a shadow in the air,
A bald eagle, with talons sharp and rare,
A rival for the cliffs and all its prey,
A challenge to the peregrine's domain.

And so the battle rages on and on,
A fight for life, a test of strength and brawn,
The falcon swoops and strikes with all its might,
Defending its nest, with all its flight.

In the end, the peregrine reigns supreme,
A champion of the cliffs, a warrior's dream,
A symbol of courage and grit and pride,
A triumph of nature, in the wild divide.

Love the Rain

Rain, how I love thee,
A soothing sound, a sight to see.
We need rain, for the earth to thrive,
But now it's coming in, and I don't know how to survive.
The drops were once a welcome sight,
But now they bring me great fright.

The roof is leaking, and the water pours in,
And I wonder how, this problem to begin.
The rain is essential, for all life to grow,
But now it's causing damage, that's hard to show.
I love the rain, but now I fear,
That it's causing damage, that's hard to bear.

The water is relentless, and it won't subside,
As it pours through the roof, and I try to hide.
I need help, to fix this leak,
Before the water destroys, all that we seek.
For rain is a blessing, that we all need,
But when it causes harm, it's hard to concede.

We need to find a way, to repair the roof,
And to protect our home, from the rain that's proof.
For rain is essential, for all that we hold dear,
But we must find balance, and we must show fear.
Of the damage it can cause, when it's too much to bear,
And find solutions, that show we care.

Rain, how I love thee,
Your gentle drops, a symphony.
The way you cleanse the earth, and bring new life,
Is a thing of beauty, a true delight.
But now the rain, it comes with a fury,
The water seeping through, with a hurry.

I don't know what to do, as it floods my home,
And I feel so lost, and so alone.
For the rain, it was once a blessing,
But now it feels like a curse, that needs addressing.
The water pouring in, with a relentless force,
Leaves me feeling overwhelmed, and filled with remorse.

But I know that the rain, it is not to blame,
For it is a natural force, that cannot be tamed.
It is our homes and our buildings, that must be made strong,
To withstand the rain, and keep us from harm.

So I will weather this storm, with strength and with grace,
And seek the help I need, to keep my home in its place.
For rain, it is a gift, that we so desperately need,
And I will learn to love it, once again, indeed.

Cantalloc Aqueducts

In the heart of a desert, mysteries lie,
The Cantalloc Aqueducts, a marvel so high,
Built by Nazca hands, so long ago,
An ancient secret, water's flow.
In valleys of Taruga, Nazca, Las Trancas' crest,
Forty-six aqueducts, a testament of the best,
Thirty-two still thriving, a legacy to share,
A pre-Inca marvel, crafted with care.
Beneath the surface, deep they run,
Twelve meters down, a journey begun,
With slab stones and huarango trunks they're made,
A testament to skill, that shall not fade.
The puquios stand, thirty-five in all,
Spiral shafts of air, a system to enthrall,
For cleaning, conservation, and water's embrace,
A testament to wisdom, in this arid place.
Against the droughts, a battle waged,
The people of Nazca, their thirst assuaged,
Their knowledge vast, a skill so rare,
An irrigation system, with none to compare.
Today the waters still flow, crops to sustain,
Corn, cotton, beans, and potatoes, life's refrain,
A treasure of Peru, a secret unveiled,
The Cantalloc Aqueducts, where mastery has prevailed.

Reviving the Cantalloc Legacy: Modern Sustainable Water Capture
Systems Inspired by Ancient Engineering

The Cantalloc Aqueducts, an ancient and efficient hydraulic
engineering marvel built by the Nazca culture (200 AD - 700 AD)
in Peru, have stood the test of time and continue to inspire awe in
modern hydrogeologists and sustainability experts. This study aims
to investigate the potential of incorporating the innovative principles
of the Cantalloc Aqueducts into contemporary sustainable water

capture systems. By analyzing the ingenious use of subterranean channels, slab stones, huarango trunks, and spiral-shaped puquios for ventilation, cleaning, and water collection, we seek to adapt these ideas to address present-day water scarcity challenges.

Our research employs a multidisciplinary approach, combining historical, archaeological, and hydrogeological data to understand the Cantalloc Aqueducts' design principles and functionality. We then propose a modern sustainable water capture system that integrates the key lessons from these ancient structures. This system is expected to maximize groundwater capture, minimize evaporation, and enhance water management practices in arid regions, while reducing environmental impact and promoting ecological resilience.

Through the revitalization of the Cantalloc legacy, we aim to contribute to the global efforts towards sustainable water management and explore innovative solutions that combine ancient wisdom with contemporary engineering for the benefit of present and future generations.

Spring Arrives

As winter recedes, and the season renews,
The hillsides awaken, adorned in bright hues,
An emerald mantle, the earth gently clad,
As springtime emerges, the world's heart, unclad.

Lupines and poppies, they dance in the breeze,
A jubilant choir, in nature's grand frieze,
They paint the horizon with colors so bold,
A symphony of life, a story untold.

The cleanse of the spring, a promise, a vow,
To rejuvenate hearts, to nature, we bow,
For in the sweet blossoms, the wildflowers' refrain,
We find a new hope, a solace from pain.

As petals unfurl, like banners they soar,
A testament to life, a pledge to restore,
The valleys and meadows, once dormant and still,
Now burst into life, as if by sheer will.

Each flower, a beacon, a symbol of grace,
A testament to renewal, in this sacred space,
The hillsides ablaze, a mosaic of fire,
In the wild, untamed beauty, our spirits aspire.

For in the explosion of color, a message is found,
A whisper of hope, a world unbound,
In the promise of spring, new horizons we trace,
As we walk hand in hand, through the wildflowers' embrace.

Two Seas

Two seas, they meet but do not mix,
A wondrous sight, a scene that truly tricks.
The line between them, clear as day,
A boundary that neither does betray.

Fresh water, from rivers and glaciers cold,
With lower salinity, a story yet untold.
It rushes forward, with a purpose so true,
But the ocean, with its might, does not misconstrue.

Where the seas meet, a wondrous sight,
Two worlds apart, yet side by side.
Their waters, different in every way,
Meet and greet, but never play.

The two come together, but stay apart,
With separate identities, a work of art.
The colors, they blend, in a dance sublime,
But they remain distinct, never to combine.

It's a lesson for us, as we journey through life,
That differences exist, and they can be rife.

And in this wonder, we can see,
A metaphor for life's diversity.
Though we may be different, like the seas,
We can coexist, and thrive, with ease.

Patterns

Life is a journey, a fractal mystery,
Full of wonder, and moments that can be slippery.
We've been taught to see it as a competition,
A never-ending battle, a struggle, and a mission.

But there's a theory that says that's not true,
It speaks of cooperation, and a different point of view.
As we look at the fractal character of evolution,
We see a pattern of cooperation, a different solution.

The elements in the geometry work together,
A grand symphony, an orchestra, we're all here in the weather.
Each part unique, but no part too small,
All contribute, as we dance to evolution's call.
The struggle and fight for survival may exist,
But they're not the whole picture, not all that exists.
Cooperation is the key, the secret to life's flow,
A grand tapestry, with beauty and balance in tow.

If you embrace this perspective,
And work together, and not forget,
That in the grand scheme of things, we're all in this together,
A shared journey, where we help each other weather.

CHAPTER 3

Love and Joy and Being Human

The Same in Different Fonts

In a world of words and letters combined,
Two souls discovered what made them aligned,
Distinct in their essence, yet bound as one,
United by serifs, their journey begun.
One danced in the curve of an elegant script,
The other stood firm, a bold typeface equipped,
Their stories entwined, like ink on a page,
Two fonts intertwining, through love and through rage.
Calligraphy whispered, a tender embrace,
While block letters anchored, providing a base,
Each held their own beauty, both separate and true,
But when intertwined, a new language they drew.
In the hearts and minds, emotions would surge,
As the words they crafted would gracefully merge,
They spoke of their love, and the world understood,
That two fonts together, create something good.
Through trials and triumphs, their bond grew strong,
Their voices harmonized, like a really good song,
For they found in each other, what they'd sought all along,
The counterpoint to their melody, where they belong.
In the vast sea of letters, where stories are spun,
Two fonts found their unity, a harmony won,
No longer alone, in a world black and white,
Together they painted, with love's vibrant light.

Blue Moon

The blue moon rises in the sky,
A sight that fills my heart with sigh,
As I gaze up at its wondrous light,
It brings back memories, so bright.
I remember the night, so clear,
When I saw you standing near,
Under the blue moon's gentle glow,
You were smiling, a radiant show.
We stood there, in the moon's embrace,
With a grin that lit up your face,
I saw you standing there alone,
A stoic wonder, like none I'd known.
The blue moon shone down on you,
As if to say, "I see you too",
And in that moment, I knew,
That I was meant to be with you.
I spoke to you, with a heart that raced,
Hoping that my love would be embraced.
And as the blue moon shone above,
We fell in love, under the moon above,
Under its gentle, calming light,
We found each other, on that magical night.
Now every time the blue moon rises high,
I think of you, my heart's delight,

The Painter

The canvas, a portal, a door to the mind,
Where fables are born, and destinies twined,
And in these vibrant landscapes, one can see,
The power of art, the soul set free.

I am the painter, the weaver of dreams,
Merging the abstract with nature's themes,
A dance of colors, both vivid and bright,
My canvas, a tapestry of hope and of blight.

In strokes and lines, I capture the soul,
Of landscapes and faces, a world to behold,
The whispers of trees, the laughter of streams,
Are all held within my intricate schemes.

My brush, it speaks, in hues and shades,
A language unspoken, where time never fades,
The tales of the wind, the sun's gentle kiss,
A world beyond words, a moment of bliss.

From chaos and order, my paintings arise,
A fusion of elements, where earth meets the skies,
A symphony of color, a delicate ballet,
The birth of new worlds, where dreams come to play.

And sometimes, these paintings, they come alive,
As stories unfold, and emotions revive,
A spark in the heart, a tear in the eye,
These living masterpieces, they make spirits fly.

For within each stroke, each careful blend,
Lies a tale untold, a message to send,
A journey of love, of loss, and of strife,
A testament to the beauty of life.

I am the painter, the dreamer, the muse,
A witness to life, its colors and hues,
Through my creations, I set free,
The stories beyond the brush, for all to see.

Cherokee Aerospace Engineer

To the stars through the stars,
A journey of the Cherokee's lore,
A story of hardships and scars,
Of how humans arrived on Earth's shore.

Mary Golda Ross, a trailblazer,
The first Native aerospace engineer,
Her successes attributed to her heritage,
The Cherokee tradition of equal education, sincere.

Through the top-secret team she planned,
The early years of space exploration,
Her brilliance and knowledge at hand,
Led to great achievements and admiration.

Her story inspires and empowers,
The importance of education and culture,
Of breaking barriers and climbing towers,
To reach for the stars, to the future.

As the Cherokee people gather,
To showcase their shared history and lifeways,
Through storytelling, music, and art of wonder,
Their culture thrives and forever stays.

To those who can't join in person,
Watch the webcast and witness,
The beauty of Cherokee's tradition,
Their resilience and strength, a true greatness.

When we look up to the stars,
We can remember the journey from afar,
Through hardships, we reach for the skies,
To the stars through the stars, our spirits arise.

Mark Twain

In the realm of words and rhyme, Mark Twain once spoke of a paradigm, Where the reader's mind soars free, And the illiterate, shackled be.

Yet in the halls of wisdom vast,
A truth unveiled, a shadow cast,
The man who reads not, stands akin, To him who cannot read within.
With boundless books, like treasure troves, Awaiting hands that seek and rove,
The one who shuns their golden light, Forfeits wisdom's endless flight.
No greater loss than to ignore,
The boundless worlds that lie in store,
For words, like keys, unlock the door,
To knowledge, dreams, and so much more.
But he who fears the written page,
Shall dwell within a self-made cage,
For when the mind's own wings are clipped, The soul in darkness stays eclipsed.
So heed the words of Twain so wise,
And let the love of books arise,
For in their pages, we shall find,
The answers to leaving questions behind.

Internalizer

In the realm of hearts and minds, there lies a great divide,
Between those who internalize, and those who can't abide.
The quiet ones, the loud, the bold, the mute,
Each bearing burdens, seeking solace in their own pursuit.

The internalizers hide their fears, tuck their pain away,
A labyrinth of secret rooms, where emotions sway.
In quiet contemplation, they nurse their tender hearts,
Unraveling their threads of thought, like intricate works of art.

They seek solace in the shadows, where whispers softly gleam,
A refuge from the chaos, where thoughts can dance and dream.
Though silence often cloaks them, in the stillness, they find peace,
For deep within the quiet, a healing light's released.

The externalizers, on the other hand, wear their hearts as shields,
With every beat, they speak their truth, emotions unconcealed.
They lay their feelings bare, a rainbow in the sky,
A vibrant tapestry of words, unafraid to cry.

They seek connection, sharing pain, as hearts join in refrain,
A symphony of empathy, where sorrow's not in vain.
In speaking out their anguish, they find solace in the sound,
A chorus of compassion, where healing love abounds.

But whether we internalize or choose to wear our hearts,
Our needs converge, a common ground, where healing love departs.
For in the dance of life, we seek connection, truth, and peace,
A shared embrace, where both may find their own emotional release.

Remember and not forget, as we wander in the dark,
That we all need love and understanding, to ignite that healing spark.
For in the end, it matters not, how we choose to cope,
As long as we reach out, and find solace in love's hope.

Jacqueline's Race for Compassion

In a race of grit and determination,
One athlete stood, a symbol of inspiration,
Jacqueline Nyetipei Kiplimo, a name we hold dear,
For the compassion she showed, in a moment sincere.
At the Zheng-Kai Marathon, in the year twenty-ten,
A tale of true kindness, we'll remember again,
For amidst the fierce struggle, she found something more,
A chance to show love, to even the score.
A double amputee, his strife plain to see,
Struggling to drink, amid the race's melee,
But Jacqueline, in that moment, saw not a chance,
To leave him behind, to further advance.
From the sixth mile to the twenty-third, side by side,
She ran with him, their spirits allied,
At each watering station, her assistance she gave,
A gesture of empathy, both tender and brave.
Though her pace was slowed, and her victory delayed,
She chose compassion, a choice unswayed,
A second-place finish, ten thousand dollars foregone,
For the warmth in her heart, like the break of the dawn.
Jacqueline's story, a testament to grace,
A reminder that kindness can transcend any race,
Her selflessness teaches, in moments most trying,
That true leadership's found, when we're selflessly vying.
Honor her spirit, her unwavering stand,
For in each act of kindness, we strengthen love's hand,
For when we choose empathy, over trophies and gold,
We create a world better, a story untold.

My Eye is the Camera Lens

My eye is the camera, so keen and bright,
It captures images with a steady sight.
My brain are the dials and buttons, so precise,
Adjusting light and color with expert eyes.
Together they work in perfect harmony,
Capturing moments that are fleeting and free.
A look, a smile, a shadow, a beam of light,
All frozen in time, before they take flight.
And on the canvas or paper, they take on a new form,

A masterpiece created, a beauty born.
The traps that capture these moments in time,
Are the vessels that hold them, forever sublime.
For every stroke of the brush, every line on the page,
Brings to life the image, the story, the sage.
And though the moment may have long since passed,
It lives on in the artwork, made to last.

We cherish the moments we imagine and see,
And capture them, for all eternity.
For through the lens of our eyes, and the dials in our brain,
We can create beauty, that will forever remain.

When Film was King

Once upon a time, when film was king,
The world of music and film would sing.
And those who devoted their lives to this art,
Would capture the beauty of the world in their heart.
With cameras in hand and a steady eye,
They'd capture the landscape, the trees, and the sky.

Each shot was precious, each moment divine,
They'd wait for hours for the perfect time.
The light, the shadow, the texture, the hue,
Every element was carefully thought through.
For they knew that once that shutter clicked,
Their art would be forever fixed.

The darkroom was their sanctuary, their domain,
A place where their magic would come to reign.
The smell of chemicals, the sound of the water,
A place where their passion would never falter.
Their devotion to their craft was pure,
A love that would forever endure.
For they knew that in the end,
Their work would be a testament to the beauty of this land.

Now, in this digital age we call our own,
The world of photography has grown.
But those who have known the devotion of film,
Will forever hold onto the magic within.

My Voice is my Message

My voice is the message, the words they seek,
A powerful force, that can make the heart speak.
It carries ideas, emotions, and dreams,
A vessel that carries the soul's very seams.
Like a bird on a breeze, it soars through the air,
Carrying with it, the weight of a prayer.

A melodic journey, floating in space,
An expression of beauty, a moment of grace.
With each breath I take, and each word I speak,
I offer a piece of myself, that's unique.
A story to tell, a truth to be heard,
A message of hope, that longs to be shared.
For in the power of my voice, lies the key,
To unlock the hearts and minds, open and free.

To inspire, to uplift, to bring light to the night,
And guide them to a future, that's filled with delight.
Do not take for granted, this gift we possess,
For our voice is a treasure, that we must daily confess.
A message of hope, that can light up the night,
And bring peace to the soul, from its melodic blight.

My voice is the message, the words they seek,
The melodies that flow, the ideas that speak.
It echoes through the air, in sweet refrain,
A symphony of sound, that will never wane.

With each intonation, each rise and fall,
It weaves a tale, that captures all.
The power of language, the magic of song,
In my voice, it all belongs.
It carries a message, a truth, a dream,
A hope, a wish, a silent scream.

And in the air, it takes on a life,
A force to be reckoned with, full of strife.
For in the music, in the words, in the sound,
Lies a beauty that knows no bounds.
It speaks to the heart, the soul, the mind,
A symphony of truth, so pure and kind.

Let my voice be heard, let it be loud, let it soar,
Let it reach for the heavens, and so much more.
For in the message, in the words, in the air,
Lies a beauty that we all can share.

…I hope.

Under Pressure

Under pressure, we all have felt
The weight of expectation, new cards dealt.
To do the right thing, to look the right way
To say the right thing, day after day
We try to fit in, to meet the norm
To be accepted, in a world so warm

But sometimes, the pressure becomes too great
And we find ourselves, lost in the weight
We second-guess ourselves, and what we know
Afraid to speak up, and let our thoughts show
We conform, and blend, and lose ourself
In the endless pursuit, of more and more wealth

But pressure, it's a double-edged sword
For sometimes, it can push us forward
To be better, to strive for more
To reach new heights, and open new doors

We feel the pressure, to our own gain
To be true to ourselves, and break the chain
To do the right thing, not just for show
To look the right way, and let our true selves glow
For in the end, it's not about the norm
It's about being true, and weathering the storm
To say the right thing, from the heart and soul
And live a life, that's true and whole.

Lifting Sadness

In the halls of youth, where laughter fades,
Where dreams are worn like masquerade,
The whispers of a somber tide,
A darkness that the young can't hide.
With heavy hearts, they bear the weight,
Of sorrow's grip, a cruel fate,
A world that seems too vast, too cold,
As forty-two percent, so we're told.
In classrooms filled with wistful eyes,
Their minds are clouded, hearts disguised,
How can we help them find the key,
To unshackle chains and set them free?
For in this space, we'll start anew,
Embrace the colors, every hue,
By painting life with love and care,
In every brushstroke, light we'll share.
We'll teach them skills to navigate,
The storms that life will orchestrate,
To persevere through dark and rain,
And find the sun through clouds of pain.
We'll offer tools to build and cope,
A scaffold for their dreams and hope,
In empathy, we'll walk the mile,
To share their burden, lift their smile.
With open hearts, we'll foster trust,
In every child, we'll plant the seed,
And as they grow, they'll learn to lead.
For in their hands, the future lies,
These blooming souls, we must advise,
With love and guidance, strong and wise,
Together, we shall rise.

CHAPTER 4

Environment and Politics Collide

Sustainability is the Key

Sustainability is the key,
To a future that's bright and free.
A world where we all can thrive,
Where resources remain alive.
We must learn to live in balance,
With nature, without any malice.
For the planet to survive,
Sustainability must be revived.
A fellowship to meet our needs,
Is time well spent, indeed.
For a future that's bright and green,
Sustainability must be our theme.
We must learn to conserve,
The resources we have the nerve.

To use them wisely, not waste,
And leave a planet that's not debased.
The time to act is now,
To make sustainability our vow.
For a world that's fit to live,
Sustainability is the gift we must give.
Let's work together as a team,
To make sustainability our dream.
For a future that's bright and free,
Sustainability is the key.

Sargassum Beast

Amidst the seas, a giant stirs,
A tale of change, of doom, it murmurs.
A sargassum mass, five thousand miles wide,
A symptom of the shifts that hide.
From azure depths, it rises high,
A tangled mass, beneath the sky.
Its growth, a mystery, yet we know,
The warming seas have made it grow.
As climate shifts, the world transforms,
Unraveling threads, the earth reforms.
From melting ice to bleaching coral,
We bear witness to this global quarrel.
For in this sargassum beast, we see,
A consequence of our apathy.
The greenhouse gases that we spew,
The altered currents, temperatures askew.
A bloom of algae, verdant and vast,
A warning from a future, a message from the past.
As we seek answers to explain,
The driving force behind this emerald chain.
With every mile, it stretches wide,
The truth of climate change, we cannot hide.

A web of life, disrupted, changed,
An ecosystem, rearranged.
And so, we turn to science, to make us wise,
To understand the hows and whys.
For in this knowledge, we may find,
The keys to save the Earth, combined.
As sargassum floats on distant seas,
We must confront our own disease.
To fight the climate change that spreads,
To heal the Earth, and forge ahead.

Cleanup to the Political Standard

Environmental cleanup to the political standard,
Seems like a game that's hard to understand.
With red tape and bureaucracy in the way,
It's difficult to see the light of day.
But amidst the struggle, there is hope,
A glimmer that allows us to cope.

For there are those who fight the good fight,
And work to make things better, with all their might.
They push for change, and they demand,
That our environment deserves a stand.
They work to clean up the air and the seas,
And to protect the land, for you and for me.

It's not an easy task, but it's one we must face,
To protect our planet, our sacred space.
For the Earth is our home, and it needs our date,
We must treat it with love, and handle it with care.
We open our eyes clear, and work towards a goal,
Of a world that's healthy, and free from the toll,

Of pollution and waste, and all that harms,
A world that's full of beauty and charms.
For environmental cleanup is more than just a chore,
It's a promise we make, and a future we restore,
It's a legacy we leave, for generations to come,
And a symbol of our love, this place we call home.

The air we breathe, the water we drink,
Are all tainted, polluted, on the brink.
But hope lies in the power of the few,
Who fight for change, who stand for what is true.
The leaders should set the standard high,
But for real, not pie in the sky.

Environmental cleanup to the political standard,
A fight for our planet, we must all demand it.
To clean up the mess we've made,
And pave the way for a brighter day.
We need leaders who believe in the cause,
Who see the urgency, and don't just pause.
Who work to create policies that care,
And put the health of our planet first, everywhere.

For in the cleanup, in the change we make,
Lies a brighter future, for our planet's sake.
A future where the air is clear, the water clean,
And the earth is cared for, like a precious dream.
Look leaders in the eye, and demand real change,
For the health of our planet, we must arrange.
A brighter future, for all to see,
And a world that's filled with possibility.

The first amendment, a cornerstone of our rights,
The freedom to speak, to debate, to fight,
To express our thoughts, opinions, and beliefs,
A right that's sacred, that no one can thief.

Forever Chemicals

In a world of marvels and wonders, of progress and gain,
A shadow lingers, a poison, a silent, toxic rain.
Forever chemicals, they're called, omnipresent and dire,
An unwelcome legacy, a world set afire.
At Santa Susana Field Lab, reassurances fell flat,
"It's not like you're drinking it," they'd say, a hollow, bitter chat.
Our waterways corrupted, our future held in chains,
The consequence of negligence, as the poison still remains.

From the depths of the ocean to the peaks of mountains high,
Forever chemicals pervade, beneath our open sky.
In every corner of the earth, they're found, a stain upon the land,
An unintended price we pay, for progress's heavy hand.

In East Palestine we see, a lesson yet unlearned,
Regulators turning heads, as our home continues burned.
A cycle of indifference, a reckless, selfish game,
The cost of our environment, and our children's future claim.
What now, we ask in anguish, as we face this daunting task,
To cleanse the earth of these toxins, and remove the dreadful ash?
We must rise above our history, and the mistakes of yesterday,
To forge a cleaner, brighter path, and guide our steps away.
Let us take this moment, a turning point in time,
To fight for our environment, and the legacy we'll find.
For if we stand united, and let our voices ring,
Together we'll confront the foe, and a better world we'll bring.

Parallels

In shadows, secrets lurk and grow,
At Santa Susana, long ago,
Where silent toxins, veiled in time,
Did bear the weight of silent crime.
A slow burn, spanning seven decades' length,
Invisible, yet strong in strength.
But in Ohio's East Palestine,
A toxic tale, vinyl chloride, no longer pristine.
A train derailed, the poison spread,
On screens, the chaos, fear, and dread.

Denial swift, as if a script,
Yet truth, like water, slowly dripped.
In both these lands, the tale is told,
Of lies and toxins, young and old.
Where unseen hands have sown their seeds,
In poisoned soil, on which life feeds.
The people, rashes, throats aflame,
Their bodies the samples, but a game.
In quiet whispers, doubt was sown,

The truth unveiled, the lies unthrown.
We turned to those who should protect,
With questions, worries, hopes to detect.
Government failures point to neglect

Yet answers vague, from distant lands,
A voice named Karen, ties our hands.
In parallels and contrasts stark,
A single thread, a toxic mark.
A lesson learned, or so we pray,
That vigilance must hold its sway.

To stand as one, and call to task,
To question, probe, unmask at last.
The hidden wrongs, the slow decay,
For truth and justice, we must weigh.

The Santa Susana Charade

In shadows of The Hill,
A toxic truth, a sorrow that chills.
A cleanup stalled, a guise to keep,
The secrets buried, darkness deep.
They speak of wanting the best, they claim,
But in their hearts, a different aim.
A false façade, a twisted ploy,
Their only goal: the truth destroy.
In science, they seek not to guide,
But wield it as a shield to hide.
Not progress sought, but boundaries set,
A game to stall, a cruel bet.
And as we spin in futile strife,
The ones who win, their pockets rife.
Boeing's stocks, they rise and swell,
While neighbors suffer, trapped in hell.
The tool they wield, a vibe they shift,
A fear they sow, a toxic rift.
No longer is the muck that's feared,
But cleansing hands, the truth once cleared.
What answer lies within this maze,
When voices raised are silenced, dazed?
What hope remains to break the hold,
Of those who trade our lives for gold?
In unity, we find the key,
A chorus strong, a voice set free.
Together, we must stand as one,
To face the lies, the truth won,
No more the shadows, nor the spin,
A truth to seek, a fight to win.
For in the end, it's we who choose,
To conquer fear and break the ruse.

Looking for Answers to Cancers

In Simi Hills, where secrets lie,
A poison's spread beneath the sky.
A hidden scourge, in soil concealed,
The truth, at last, begins to yield.

Santa Susana, tainted ground,
In trichloroethylene, we've found.
A cancer threat, now brought to light,
Yet deeper fears emerge from night.

A potent force, a threat unseen,
Degreasing jets, machinery clean.
But in the wake, a toxic toll,
A creeping dread, consuming whole.

The whispers rise, a link to trace,
To Parkinson's, a trembling face.
A question posed, a chilling thought,
What have we wrought, what have we sought?

For decades passed, the use widespread,
And now we count the toll in dread.
A legacy of tainted wells,
A silent foe, in homes it dwells.

In vapors breathed, in water sipped,
Our lives entwined, our futures gripped.
From factories to housing sites,
A toxic dance, a wrong to right.

Awake, we must, to silent cries,
To avert our gaze, no more, from ties.
For in this truth, we hold the key,
To heal the land, and set us free.

No longer blind to ancillary,
We listen, learn, and act with clarity.
In Santa Susana's tortured tale,
We forge a path, a truth unveiled.

Change the Audience

In the Golden State of California's reign,
Lies a tale of whispers, poison, and disdain,
The DTSC, they call themselves with pride,
But deep within, dark secrets reside.
Beneath the Santa Susana Field Lab's glow,
The people suffer, the toxins flow,
Yet the DTSC, defenders they claim to be,
Shield the polluters, but not you and me.
A strategy devised, cunning and sly,
Erase the voices that question and pry,
Replace them with those who seek but a treat,
Donuts they crave, their inquiries deceit.
But voices of truth can't be silenced for long,
Like resilient flowers, they'll rise and grow strong,
Battling the shadows that corruption brings,
Demanding answers and change that springs.
The government's power, bestowed by us all,
Turned against us, creating a wall,
Control and erase, to maintain their rule,
Casting a veil, as the people they fool.
"It's not like you're drinking it," DTSC staff say,
But forever chemicals lurk, in our lives every day,
Invisible enemies, infiltrating our core,
As we demand answers, seeking something more.
What say you now, Sirs? with eyes open wide,
Unmask the deception, bring truth to light,
Together we'll stand, as one we'll fight,
For the justice we seek, in our eternal plight.

I know we aren't as one,
That much even I can see.
We are indeed as divided as can be,
But now the divided are divided,
So while it used to be the plan to be,
The unofficial script offered up by everyone you hear or see,

It will be their undoing,
Just more of their own insanity
Since the divided have their own ideas and thoughts,
And too many of them cannot be bought.
While this is clearly not the finale,
You've backed the wrong horse,
and with no remorse.
The truth will rise finally,
Of course, of course,

AUTHOR'S NOTE

Pluralism and reductionism, as two philosophical concepts that differ in their approach to understanding the complexity of reality. At Santa Susana, it can be explained by comparing the understanding a person has who has read the flyer that brought them to the hearing, versus someone who has read nearly all the reports which they purposely make in thousand page increments. If you have to read a thousand pages to understand, or a one-page flyer, you're probably gonna read the flyer.

In philosophy, they each have unique implications when applied to various disciplines, including politics and the functioning of democracies, and the regulation of pollutants both sudden and long-term.

Pluralism posits that there are multiple, equally valid perspectives or explanations for a given phenomenon. It embraces diversity and acknowledges that no single perspective can capture the entirety of a complex reality. In the context of democracies, pluralism is often linked to the notion that a healthy democracy requires a diversity of opinions, values, and beliefs, as well as the protection of minority rights.

Reductionism, on the other hand, is the belief that complex phenomena can be explained by breaking them down into simpler, more fundamental components. It seeks to find a single underlying principle or set of principles that can account for everything. In politics, reductionism might manifest as the belief that a single ideology or policy approach is sufficient to address all societal issues.

Democracies can be faulted in the wake of these philosophical approaches in several ways:

1. Oversimplification: Reductionism in democracies can lead to oversimplification of complex issues, resulting in the

implementation of policies that may not adequately address the true nature of the problem. This can lead to unintended consequences and exacerbate existing issues.

2. Lack of representation: A reductionist approach in politics may result in the marginalization of minority perspectives, leading to a lack of representation and a disregard for the diverse needs of the population. This can undermine the very foundations of democracy, which thrive on the inclusion of multiple perspectives.

3. Polarization: When pluralism is not adequately valued, democracies may become more polarized as people cling to their own singular beliefs and ideologies. This can lead to political gridlock, increased partisanship, and a decreased willingness to compromise or collaborate across ideological lines.

4. Suppression of dissent: In some cases, a reductionist approach in a democracy may lead to the suppression of dissenting voices in the pursuit of a single, unified narrative. This can stifle free speech, hinder innovation, and undermine the democratic process.

Democracies can be faulted when they either fail to appreciate the value of pluralism and the importance of diverse perspectives or when they rely too heavily on reductionist approaches to address complex issues. Striking a balance between these two philosophical stances is essential for fostering a healthy, inclusive, and effective democratic society.

The concepts of pluralism and reductionism, as well as their implications for democracies have fascinated me for a very long time, but never like it does now. These are well-established in the philosophical and political science literature.

If you are interested in further reading on pluralism, reductionism, and their implications for democratic societies, you can explore the following sources:

1. Berlin, Isaiah. (2002). "Liberty: Incorporating Four Essays on Liberty." Oxford University Press.

2. Churchland, Paul M. (1988). „Matter and Consciousness." MIT Press.

3. Connolly, William E. (2005). "Pluralism." Duke University Press.

4. Dahl, Robert A. (1998). "On Democracy." Yale University Press.

5. Nagel, Ernest. (1961). "The Structure of Science: Problems in the Logic of Scientific Explanation." Harcourt, Brace & World.

Climate Change UN IPCC Report

Upon this fragile sphere we dwell,
A tale of woe and change to tell,
As Earth, besieged by human hand,
Awaits the fate that we command.

The IPCC, they raise the alarm,
For in our wake, we've caused great harm,
A legacy of smoke and fire,
The climate's tipping point, now dire.

In years unmatched in history,
We've shaped the Earth, transformed the sea,
Our actions left a wound so deep,
The planet sleeps as ecosystems weep.

The goal of one-point-five degrees,
Now fading fast like autumn leaves,
For we have failed to grasp the reins,
And now face floods, drought, endless pains.

Our leaders gather, pledging change,
But time runs short, the hour is strange,
As nations lag in their pursuit,
The Earth's demise, a bitter fruit.

Inequalities divide the land,
The rich, the poor, must understand,
That unity and swifter pace,
Can save our home, this fragile space.

The tools we have, the knowledge vast,
To heal the scars of our tainted past,
But time is fleeting, sands run thin,
We must act now, or face Earth's din.

António Guterres cries the call,
To nations, leaders, one and all,
To hasten strides, cut emissions fast,
To save our future, heal the past.

No more the coal, the oil, the gas,
For in their wake, destruction's mass,
Together, now, we forge a path,
To mend our home, avert Earth's wrath.

This report, a guide to heed,
A final chance to change, indeed,
For in our hands, the world now lies,
To claim our fate, or face demise.

Intrepid Outliers

In the realm of data, where numbers abide,
Intrepid outliers, they often reside,
A deviation from norms, a curious case,
In people, in toxins, and in cyberspace.
People who dare to walk their own path,
Defying convention, resisting the wrath,
Of the mainstream, that seeks to contain,
The brilliance that shines in each renegade's vein.
In data they dwell, far from the crowd,
A statistical enigma, their presence unbowed,
The anomaly that challenges what's understood,
The exception that reshapes, the misunderstood.
In toxic contamination, the truth they unveil,
The scarce few anomalies, in a world that's grown pale,
Exposing the dangers that lie beneath,
A harbinger of peril, a warning to bequeath.
Yet narratives spun, in a world of deceit,
May silence these outliers, make them obsolete,
The story they tell, often dismissed,
In the name of convenience, or the turn of a wrist.
But the intrepid outliers, they hold the key,
To unmask the unknown, to set the truth free,
For in their divergence, in their solitary stance,
Lies the power to question, to give truth a chance.
Pay attention and listen, to the whispers they share,
For the intrepid outliers, bring wisdom so rare,
Their stories, like beacons, cut through the night,
Guiding us forward, to a future more bright.

Climate Change

In the realm of shifting seasons, where the climate's fate is tried,
We see the droughts and floods converging, nature's balance set aside.
The skeptics cry, "La Niña!", as if it quells the fear,
But every towel upon the floor tells a tale we're loath to hear.
The tarps are stretched and taut, their burden to withstand,
Yet the deluge knows no pity, as it sweeps across the land.
In the midst of chaos, we yearn for solace and reprieve,
A respite from the torrents, and the doubts that we perceive.
The fickle answers offered, like whispers in the wind,
Do little to console us, as our patience wears thin.
We seek a peaceful open mind, a shelter from the storm,
A haven where our hearts may rest, and our weary souls transform.

But climate change persists, its truth cannot be swayed,
By those who would deny it, or the games that they have played.
The earth it speaks, a tale of woe, of imbalance and of strife,
A warning to humanity, to protect our fragile life.
Rise high above the fray, and face the truths we find,
Acknowledge that the world we love is no longer well-aligned.
Together, let us work for change, and embrace the challenge posed,

To heal the wounds upon the earth, and the legacy we've chose.
In this journey toward redemption, we'll find our peace of mind,
A unity of purpose, that leaves the narrow-minded behind.
For it's in our shared endeavor, to protect the world we hold,
That we'll conquer fear and doubt, and write a story to be told.

Amidst the whispers of the wind, a warning calls us near,
A tale of climate's shifting tides, and the future we should fear.
As droughts extend their gnarled hands, and rivers cease to flow,
The skeptics scoff at nature's wrath, and let La Niña grow.
They claim it's but a passing phase, a fleeting, false alarm,
And yet, our world's transforming, as the storms around us swarm
and swarm.

With every towel upon the floor, to soak the floods that rise,
We bear the brunt of nature's ire, beneath uncertain skies.
The tarps they give, they offer solace, but no relent we find,
For in the face of fickle answers, we seek a truth unblind.
Our hearts yearn for a peaceful state, an open, tranquil mind,
But the tempests that surround us, leave us feeling far confined.
As waters surge and forests burn, we look for reasons why,
The shifting climate shapes our world, as the clouds adorn the sky.
The dance of La Niña taunts us, a riddle to unwind,
And in its complex patterns, we hope for answers to find.
In the chaos of the storm, let us strive for clarity,
Acknowledge the impending change, and the perils that we see.
For only through awareness, can we hope to stem the tide,
And in the face of trite answers, a peaceful mind we'll find.
Let us stand together, united in our quest,
To face the threats of climate change, and put our hearts to test.
With open minds and hopeful hearts, we'll navigate the storm,
And in the strength of unity, a brighter world we'll form.

Going EV?

In the shadows of a world in flux, a whisper echoes clear,
A call to change our ways, to quell the threats that we hold dear.
The climate shifts, a warning sign, that we must leave behind,
The oil that sleeps beneath the earth, a relic of the past unkind.
As we embrace electric charge, to power cars anew,
Resistance rears its stubborn head, and questions what we do.
They blame the batteries we build, with fingers quick to point,
And claim concern for earth and life, yet oil's toll they do discount.
The mining of exotic metals, a challenge to be faced,
With proper management, we strive to keep our hands unchased.
No blood upon our diamonds, as we forge a path ahead,
Innovation and compassion, the values we'll embed.
We must advance, both hand in hand, united in our goal,
To foster independence, while collaboration takes control.
Protect the earth, its people too, and wildlife we adore,
For in their preservation, we secure a world we can explore.
A future built on cleaner means, to move and breathe and be,
Free from chains of blackened gold, and smog that blinds our plea.
Together we'll discover, the solutions that we crave,
A harmony with nature, in a world that we shall save.
We can let the winds of progress blow, and lead us to the light,
Innovation, care, and hope, our compass in the night.
We'll stand against the naysayers, and the doubts that they may sow,
For in our hearts and minds, the seeds of change will grow.

Toxic Food Web

In the shadows of the moonlit night,
A silent hunter takes its flight,
The Great Horned Owl, with eyes so bright,
A guardian of nature's sacred rite.

But deep within the forest's fold,
A tale of sorrow does unfold,
A toxic chain, its grip takes hold,
And on this hunter, takes its toll.

The poison spread by human hands,
To rid their homes of rodent bands,
In ignorance, they fail to understand,
The damage wrought upon the land.

The poisoned prey, a fateful bite,
Seals the owl's untimely plight,
Weakened wings, and fading light,
The hunter's end draws near, in sight.

In the grasp of pain, it finds its rest,
Emaciated, weak, distressed,
The gentle hands of those who tend,
To heal the wounded, broken friend.

Yet, for this owl, 'twas all too late,
A victim of a cruel fate,
A life cut short by careless hate,
A solemn truth we contemplate.

If we could finally learn from this somber tale,
To tread more lightly, to prevail,
In harmony with nature's scale,
And choose the path that leaves no trail.

For in our choices, we possess,
The power to heal, or to oppress,
Let wisdom guide our hearts' address,
To cherish life, and coalesce.

Toxins

In a world besieged by toxins and waste,
The battle we face, no moment to waste,
To safeguard the earth, our home and our hearth,
For the sake of our kin, the future's rebirth.

Industries rise, their ambitions, they soar,
But blind to the damage, they choose to ignore,
The rivers they poison, the air that they taint,
The lives they endanger, a picture we paint.

We fight for the truth, with conviction we stand,
Demanding a change, a shift in command,
For the billionaires, the blinded elite,
Cannot grasp that their greed leads to defeat.

Their pensions, a false sense of security,
A veil to disguise the impending impurity,
But the toxins they've spread, like venom, they seep,
Into body and soul, a harvest we'll reap.

The brain, it corrodes, the heart, it desponds,
As we struggle to break the unyielding bonds,
The fight to protect, to purify, to defend,
A battle we'll wage, until the bitter end.

We must convince them, to see the truth clear,
The legacies tainted, the cost they hold dear,
For the choices they make, the cover-ups sown,
Will follow their families, to the generations unknown.

United, we stand, a force to be reckoned,
With voices that echo, a message to beckon,
The right thing to do, the right thing to demand,
A world free of toxins, a future to remand.

Our call to action, a beacon of light,
To break through the darkness, to conquer the blight,
For in unity, we find our strength and our might,
To protect our environment, we'll continue the fight.

CHAPTER 5

Introspection

Three Pieces of Me

In the tapestry of my soul, three threads entwine,
Distinct and vibrant, each its own design.
One bold, unyielding, a force to be known,
The second uncertain, a quiet, whispered tone.

The third, ever yearning, in knowledge seeks to grow,
To learn and connect, with the world below.
Together they weave, a complex dance of three,
Creating the fabric of the person that is me.

The boldness I carry, a fire deep inside,
A passion for life, with courage as my guide.
Fearlessly, I challenge the world that I face,
Through storms and battles, I embrace my place.

Yet uncertainty lingers, a soft, wavering breeze,
A whisper of doubt in my mind's endless seas.
At times it may stifle, but it also can teach,
A humbling reminder, life's lessons beseech.

And in the yearning, a hunger so profound,
For knowledge and growth, connections unbound.
A pursuit of wisdom, for life's truths I seek,
In the hearts of others, in the words they speak.

These three pieces of me, in harmony they dance,
A composition of life, in each step and each glance.
Embracing the bold, the uncertain, and the wise,
Together they form me, a mosaic of life's tries.

Undisputed Loss

Loss is a heavy burden to bear,
A weight that sits heavy, and hard to repair.
For when we lose someone we love,
It feels like a war, raging within and above.
Death is a thief, that takes without reason,
Leaving us to cope, in the darkest season,
I seriously, can't even.

We search for answers, but find none to heal,
The ache in our hearts, that we can't conceal.
And guilt, it creeps in, like a poison in our veins,
A weight we can't shake, that causes so much pain.
We ask ourselves, what more could we have done,
And try to untangle, the knots that have begun.
But in loss, there's a love that never fades,
A bond that time, can never degrade.
For our loved ones live on, in the memories we keep,
And in the love, that we continue to reap.
We honor our heroes, and remember their light,
And keep them close, in our hearts and sight.

For though they may be gone, they are never far,
And we can love them always, right where we are.
Let's celebrate their lives, with laughter and tears,
And hold onto their love, through the coming years.
For though they may be missed, the love we share remains,
A bond unbreakable, that nothing can restrain.
Let's keep our heroes close, in our hearts and minds,
And honor their memory, with love that forever binds.
For in loss, there's a love that never fades,
A bond unbreakable, that time can never degrade.

When death comes, it's not just a loss,
It's a rift in the fabric, that carries a cost.

For we're separated, from those we love,
And we nearly go to war, with ourselves, trying to rise above.
Guilt and grief, they intertwine,
A knot in our hearts, that's hard to unwind.
For we can't help but feel, that we should have done more,
And we're left with a yearning, that cuts to the core.

But in the midst of the pain, we can find a way,
To keep our loved ones close, every night and day.
For though they may be gone, they still live on,
In the memories we hold, and the love that's strong.
We don't have to untangle the guilt, or let go of the past,
For we can hold onto the love, and make it last.
Our heroes live on, in the stories we tell,
And the lessons they taught us, that we hold so well.

Honor their memory, and keep them close,
With every thought, and every prose.
For death may separate us, but love keeps us strong,
And our heroes will always be with us, where they belong.
In the end, it's not about the guilt or the pain,
But about the love that remains.
For we may lose our heroes, but their love never dies,
And we'll stay in love with them, forever, as time flies.

We must let go of the guilt, and the pain,
And embrace the love that will always remain.
For though death may separate us, it cannot sever,
The bond we share, with our heroes forever.

When we lose someone dear to us,
A chasm opens, deep and treacherous.
We find ourselves alone and lost,
In a world without them, and a heart with frost.
Death separates us from our loved ones,
A final act, that can't be undone.

We feel a weight, so hard to bear,
And we nearly go to war with ourselves, trying to repair.
Guilt and pain, they intertwine,
A web so intricate, hard to unwind.
We second-guess ourselves, and what we've done,
Thinking we could have saved, our loved one.

But loss, it's not about blame or guilt,
It's about the love we've built.
A bond that lasts beyond this life,
And stays with us, through every strife.
For even though they may be gone,
Our love for them, it still lives on.

In making us who we are today,
And guiding us, through every step of the way.
We can stay in love with our heroes forever,
For in our hearts, their love will never wither.
And though they may have left this world,
Their love for us, it will never be unfurled.

The Story Teller

The story teller weaves her tale,
A master of the craft.
She paints a picture with her words,
And brings our story's final draft.

The story teller is a guide,
A mentor and a friend.
A light that shines upon our path,
A beacon to the end.

With every sentence, every phrase,
She captures our attention.
Her words like magic, cast a spell,
We are lost in rapt redemption.

The story teller has an eye,
That watches all our lives unfold.
She sees the beauty and the pain,
The tales that must be told.

She takes our joys, our fears, our dreams,
And turns them into gold.
She finds the meaning in our lives,
And shares it with the world, so bold.

She brings us laughter, brings us tears,
She takes us on a journey far.
She opens up our hearts and minds,
And shows us who we truly are.

The story teller is a gift,
A treasure to behold.
She gives us words to live by,
And stories that never grow old.

So listen well to what she says,
And let her tales unfold.
For in the story teller's hands,
Our lives seem to glisten like gold.

A story teller sits amongst us,
A quiet observer of our lives.
A sage who sees beyond the surface,
To the struggles and the strife.

With words that paint a vivid picture,
They weave a tale so clear and true.
Their voice a beacon in the darkness,
Guiding us through life anew.

They tell of love and loss and longing,
Of joy and hope and pain.
And in their stories, we find solace,
A light that helps us see again.

Their words can move us to tears or laughter,
Make us question all we know.
For in their tales, we find the answers,
And the courage to let go.

We listen to them if we're so inclined,
And heed their words of their wisdom.
For in their stories, we will find,
The truth that lies within them.

And as we journey through this life,
The story teller's words will guide.
The eye that watches over us,
The light that's always by our side.

The story teller, with eyes that see
The world as it is, and as it could be.
With a voice that carries tales untold,
And the power to make our hearts unfold.
Through words and gestures, the story teller weaves,
A tapestry of tales that never leaves.

Time is a Thief

We all wish to capture time,
To hold it still, and make it ours.
To keep those fleeting moments close,
And use them as guiding stars.
For time, it moves so fast it seems,
A blur of days and weeks and years.
And as we struggle to keep up,
We long to slow it down, and hold it dear.

But even though we can't stop time,
We can capture moments, and make them ours.
A picture, a memory, a feeling held close,
A path remembered in the darkest hours.
For in these moments, we find ourselves,
A piece of who we are, and where we've been.
We hold them close, and cherish them,
And use them to guide us, again and again.

We may not be able to hold time still,
But we can keep these moments close at hand.
A reminder of the beauty in our lives,
A way back to our path, to understand.
So capture time, in all its fleeting glory,
And keep those moments close to heart.
For they will guide you through the years,
And have helped you from the very start.

We capture memories in photos, in words, in art,
Preserving them forever in our heart.
For they are the moments that make us feel alive,
The moments that make our spirits thrive.

And in the fleeting moments of our lives,
These are memories we must strive
To capture and hold, to keep alive,
And to cherish forever as time flies.

For as we journey through our days,
These captured moments light our ways.
They remind us of love, and of life,
And help us through moments of strife.
In photographs, in letters, in keepsakes,
We capture time, before it fades.
For these are the paths that lead us back,
To the moments we've lived, and never lack.

We have to take the time and patience to capture,
These moments, at the smallest aperture
For they are the paths we follow,
To find our way back, and not feel hollow.

Time is a thief that steals away,
Moments fleeting, gone each day.
We grasp and hold, but cannot keep,
The memories we long to seep.
But there is a way to capture time,
To keep it close, a memory sublime.
A fleeting moment, forever held,
In our hearts, a story compelled.
All captured in a moment's time,
To keep us grounded, in the daily grind.
For life moves on, and time does too,
And those memories can help us through.
They guide us back to what we've known,
A path to follow, to find our way home.
So capture time, in all its forms,
The good, the bad, the calm, the storms.

For every moment, holds a key,
To the person we were, and who we'll be.
Time may be a foe, not a friend,
One we cannot control or bend.
It moves so swiftly, yet so slow,
Leaving us with regrets, we wish to forgo.
Words we speak, they can't be unsaid,
Echoes in our minds, we can't escape the dread.

The hurt they cause, the pain they bring,
Can linger on, and sting and sting.
But what if we could turn back time,
To erase the words that caused the grime.
To find the prose that makes clear,
Our meaning and intent, so very dear.
To take back the hurt, and the pain,
To start anew, without the strain.

A force for good, if we choose to see,
The beauty in the words that set us free.
Time ticks by, like the sands of the sea,
Moments fleeting, like a melody.
And yet, sometimes we wish we could erase,
The words we spoke in haste.
I wish we could take back the words we said,
And find new prose to make clear instead.

To open doors that we had closed,
And find the meaning that we had opposed.
For time is fickle, and so are we,
We speak sometimes without clarity or charity.
If we could erase the words we wish we could take back,
We'd find our way back from feeling so side tracked.
So let us backtrack, away from attack, and avoid the wrack.
And hang on to each other, like a secret code we've hacked.

Let us speak with purpose, and with love,
So that our words may be trusted, and we remain hand in glove.
And if we falter, and make mistakes,
Let us learn from them, for our own sake.
For time ticks by, and waits for none,
And in the end, to be seen will be won.

For words are powerful, with the ability to hurt,
And time can magnify the pain, that's for certain.
But if we could go back and make amends,
We could build a bridge, and be new and better friends.
For every word we say, carries weight,
And time can either heal, or seal our fate.
So let's choose our words, with care and thought,
And mend the broken bridges that we've wrought.

Adrift

In the warmth of home, we used to dwell,
A tapestry of love, a story to tell.
But shadows loom, and whispers spread,
A fraying fabric, as hearts bled.
The hearth that glowed with laughter bright,
Now flickers dim, like dying light.
How swift the tides of life can change,
Familiar faces turning strange.
Where once we stood, a family strong,
Now echoes with a bitter song.
The ties that bound, have slipped away,
Leaving hearts adrift, in cold dismay.
Lost in the maze of fractured dreams,
A family torn at fragile seams.
We search for solace, a place to rest,
But emptiness remains, our uninvited guest.
In quiet moments, memories rise,
Of sunlit smiles and lullabies.
Yet, through the tears, we find our way,
To forge new paths, come what may.
For in the storm, we'll seek the light,
To heal our wounds and mend the fight.
And though our family may have changed,
Our love endures, just rearranged.
Eventually rising from shadows cast,
To build a future from the past.
For in this journey, we shall learn,
That love's a flame that always burns.

Weight of the World

When the weight of the world feels heavy on our chest,
And the light at the end of the tunnel seems to be a jest,
When the road we've traveled seems too long and rough,
And we feel like giving up, it's all too tough.
But in that moment, we dig deep and find,
A strength we didn't know we had inside.
A resilience, a grit, a fire to fight,
And we rise from the ashes, with renewed might.

We find a new day, amidst the dark,
And we move forward, with a steady heart.
We take one step at a time, with a purpose in mind,
And we leave our doubts and fears, far behind.
For giving up is not an option, it's not who we are,
We are warriors, who have come too far.
We've faced trials and tribulations, and we've come out strong,
And we will continue to do so, as we move along.
So let us embrace the challenges, with open arms,
And find the courage to weather the storms.
For in the moment when we feel like giving up,
We dig deep and find a new day, a new chapter to write up.
We take a deep breath, and we take a step,
And we move forward, with nothing to regret.

For the moment may be tough, but we are tougher still,
And we will rise above it all, with a steadfast will.
Never give up, no matter the cost,
For the journey is long, but the reward is worth the cost.
And in the end, we'll look back, and we'll see,
The moments we thought we couldn't, we did indeed, conquer and be.

There are moments in life, when we feel like giving up,
When the weight of the world, seems too heavy to bear or sup.
Our burdens seem endless, and the path ahead unclear,

And we wonder if we have the strength, to persevere.
But in those moments, when all hope seems lost,
We must dig deep, and pay the cost.

For within us lies a strength, we never knew we had,
A resilience, that keeps us going, even when we're sad.
We must find the courage, to face the challenges ahead,
To keep moving forward, with determination instead.
For giving up is not an option, in this journey we call life,
We must find a new day, and conquer all our strife.

It's in those moments of struggle, that we grow and evolve,
And become stronger, more resilient, and more resolved.
So when we feel like giving up, we must remember this,
That we have the power, to overcome any abyss.
For the human spirit is a force, that knows no bounds,
And with determination and perseverance, we can turn our lives around.

United We Stand

We stand together, as sisters and brothers,
A family united, unlike any others.
For though our paths may differ in life,
We share a bond that's stronger than strife.
We lift each other up, in times of need,
And help each other plant new seeds.
For growth and change are not a solo game,
But a team effort, that we all claim.
And as we stand, side by side,
We don't forget, the others who reside.
For we are all connected, in this world we share,
And it's up to us, to show that we care.

To pick up those who have been knocked down,
And help them rise, to their feet once again.
We stand with our sisters, and our brothers,
But we don't forget, the others.
For we are all in this together,
And it's up to us, to make it better.
Stand together, and lift each other up,
And show the world, that we're not giving up.
For we are in this together, with a bond so strong,
And we'll keep fighting, until the fight is won.

Rhythm Unchained

In a world of rhythm, we dance to the beat,
Chained to the melody, we shuffle our feet,
That song in our head, a siren's refrain,
A call to the masses, to break from the chain.

With rose-colored glasses, we look away,
From the truth that unfolds, and the light of day,
Our vision distorted, we choose to ignore,
The corruption that reigns, and the leaders we bore.

We move to the rhythm, but do we see,
The faces of others, their humanity?
As we sway to the music, we're caught in a trance,
Blind to the world, and the unfolding dance.

But a whisper emerges, a voice that resounds,
A plea for awakening, a call that astounds,
"Unchain from the rhythm, let go of the haze,
Remove the rose-colored glasses, and set your soul ablaze."

For in the heart of the fire, our vision clears,
And we see one another, beyond the veneer,
Of difference and distance, the masks that we wear,
We find our connection, our humanity laid bare.

Together we rise, united we stand,
Against the corruption that taints our land,
No longer fooled by the rhythm's sweet spell,
We break from the chains, and the lies they compel.

With eyes wide open, we embrace the light,
And walk hand in hand, through the darkest night,
For in the truth that we share, and the love that we find,
We wake from the rhythm, and leave the chains behind.

Pain

In times of trial and pain,
You have shown such strength, time and again.
Through all the challenges life has thrown,
You have stood tall, and never been alone.
Your care for yours, so kind and true,
Is a testament to the love in you.

A love that knows no bounds or measure,
And shines through in every act of treasure.
In her time of need, you are always there,
A rock to lean on, a soul to share.
Your courage in vulnerability,
Is a beacon of hope for all to see.
For in a world that can be so harsh,
Your kindness and compassion are a balm to parched.

A reminder of the goodness in humanity,
And the beauty of selfless generosity.
So take heart, dear one, in all you do,
For your love and care are a gift so true.
And in the midst of life's storms and gales,
Your unwavering spirit never fails.

Natural Philosophy

Philosophy, a subject oft maligned,
Is criticized for the beliefs it finds.
But do they know that science's roots,
Lay deep in philosophy's pursuits?
For in the days of ancient Greece,
Philosophy and science shared a lease.
The study of the natural world,
Was called natural philosophy, unfurled.

From Aristotle to Descartes' time,
Philosophy paved science's climb.
The exploration of the universe,
Was fueled by philosophy's verse.
But now in modern times, we see,
A division between the two, it seems to be.
Science and philosophy thought apart,
But they are connected at the heart.
So criticize philosophy if you must,
But remember that science's trust,
Was built on philosophy's foundation,
The pursuit of knowledge's elevation.
We can't soon disparage philosophy's worth,
For it gave science its very birth.
The study of the natural world, you see,
Is founded on philosophy's history.

Yesterday's Horse

In the meadow of our memories, yesterday's horse stands still,
A symbol of the faults we've made, the gaps we've yet to fill.
But as the dawn of morning breaks, we're given a fresh start,
A chance to leave the past behind, and let our journey part.
Don't ride the horse of yesterday, for it bears the weight of strife,
The echoes of mistakes we've made, that haunt our waking life.
Instead, approach with open heart, a new and vibrant steed,
Embrace the day with hopeful eyes, and let your spirit lead.
With every stride we take today, we break the chains that bind,
The heavy load of yesteryear, no longer to our mind.
We gallop toward the future, with fresh expectations bright,
No longer tethered to the past, we ride into the light.
Each day a blank canvas, a chance to learn and grow,
To shed the skin of yesterday, and let the new winds blow.
We'll navigate the winding path, with hearts both brave and bold,
For every step is progress, and a chance to break the mold.
So harness the potential, of each new day's embrace,
And let the horse of yesterday, retire with love and grace.
For in the present moment, we hold the **power to rewrite,**
Our stories filled with hope and strength, and free from shadows' blight.

A Child so Bright

In the realm of youthful wonder, where dreams and laughter play,
A child of wonder resides, with a mind that lights the way.
So curious, a prodigy so bright,
A young mind with the power to touch the stars at night.
His mother watches on with pride, as he grasps the unknown,
A brilliance so remarkable, it leaves her mind full-blown.
For His comprehension stretches far beyond his years,
A tapestry of knowledge, that the universe reveres.
He delves into the mysteries, of science, math, and more,
Exploring realms of wisdom, that others may ignore.
With each new day, he conquers worlds, his intellect ablaze,
A child of boundless curiosity, in awe, we stand and gaze.
His mother's love and guidance, a beacon in his quest,
She nurtures and supports him, as he tackles every test.
In His eyes, she sees the light, a future yet untold,
A promise of potential, that in his heart, he holds.
For in this gifted child, a universe resides,
A testament to human strength, and the power that abides.
With every thought and question, he reaches for the skies,
An open young mind, a shining star, forever on the rise.

International Women's Day

On this International Women's Day we stand,
To celebrate the progress that we've made,
And honor the women who have raised their hand,
To fight for equality, unafraid.

We've come so far since suffrage days of old,
When women marched and struggled to be heard,
And yet, the journey's long, the path is bold,
As we still strive for justice, undeterred.

For though we've won some battles, it's true,
There's still a war that rages on today,
Where women fight for equal rights anew,
In every corner, every land, every way.

Raise our voices, loud and clear,
To champion the cause of every girl and woman here.

Roots

The roots that anchor us strong,
The ones who love us all along,
Through every high and every low,
They never let us go.

A bond that's formed through blood and love,
A connection that can never be shoved,
They stand beside us through thick and thin,
With them, we know we always win.

They lift us up when we are down,
And wipe away our tears and frown,
Their support is a soothing balm,
That gives us comfort, keeps us calm.

They cheer us on in all we do,
And celebrate when dreams come true,
Their love is a constant guide,
That helps us through life's ups and downs ride.

Cherish your loved ones every day,
And let them know you're here to stay,
Together, we can conquer all,
And rise above even the toughest fall.

Gen-Z

Young people, hear my words and take them in,
For you are the future that's about to begin,
But in these times of strife and great division,
It's easy to feel lost, without a clear vision.

We're told that hopelessness is what we'll know,
That our futures are destined to be low,
But let me tell you now, that's not the case,
For we have the power to create a better place.

The world around us may be filled with hate,
But we can rise above and change our fate,
We must remain diligent, focused, and strong,
For our futures are ours, and we belong.

No one can control what's yet to come,
If we remain steadfast, we'll overcome,
We'll build a world that's bright and true,
And show that hope and unity can pull us through.

So young people, rise up and take the lead,
For in your hands lies the power to succeed,
Together, we'll create a future that's bright,
Filled with hope, love, and an unwavering fight.

There's a world outside that's full of love,
Where every child is seen, heard and above
All the labels and expectations we hold,
That tell us who we should be, and what we're told.

Message from the Council of 13 Indigenous Grandmothers:

...."Your ancestors from long ago knew how to do this. They knew the power of the feminine principle... and because you carry their DNA in your body, this wisdom and this way of being is within you. Call on it. Call it up. Invite your ancestors in. As the yang-based habits and the decaying institutions on our planet begin to crumble, look up. A breeze is stirring. Feel the sun on your wings."
https://ntvho.pe/3ZW9cs0

In whispers of the ancients, wisdom weaves,
A tapestry of knowledge, long believed,
Our grandmothers of old, their voices sing,
An ode to sacred power, feminine.

From distant past, they knew the sacred way,
To balance yang with yin, keep strife at bay,
Their blood, our blood, it flows within our veins,
Their memory, our treasure, unchained.

Ancestral wisdom, now we call upon,
As shadows rise, in twilight's fading song,
We summon strength, from deep within our core,
The potent force, our grandmothers bore.

As institutions crumble, built on lies,
And yang's dominion wanes, beneath the skies,
We turn our gaze to winds that softly blow,
And spread our wings, embrace the sun's warm glow.

The breeze is stirring, whispers on the wind,
An ancient song, our lineage rescinds,
Together, we shall rise, ancestral kin,
Our planet healed, in balance once again.

So heed the call, invite your ancestors near,
Their wisdom, like the wind, shall persevere,
The feminine, in harmony, shall reign,
And guide us to a world of love, unchained.

AUTHOR'S NOTE

The phrase "If you are explaining, you are losing" implies that if someone is in a position where they have to explain their actions or ideas, it means that they are already at a disadvantage. This phrase is often used in political discourse to suggest that if a politician or public figure is forced to explain their position, they have already lost the battle for public opinion.

This phrase can be applied to political discourse because politicians often have to explain their positions on issues. If they are constantly having to defend themselves and their policies, it suggests that they are not connecting with the public and are losing the argument. In other words, if they have to explain themselves, they are already on the back foot.

The anti-intellectual movement, which has gained momentum in the US in recent years, has been criticized for dumbing down America. This movement rejects the value of intellectualism, expertise, and higher education, and instead promotes a distrust of experts and a preference for simplistic solutions to complex problems. This movement is seen as problematic because it undermines the value of critical thinking and reasoned debate, which are necessary for a healthy democracy. By rejecting expertise and dismissing complex issues, it can lead to a lack of understanding and engagement in important political issues, making it more difficult for people to make informed decisions.

Furthermore, by promoting simplistic solutions, the anti-intellectual movement can also contribute to the polarization of political discourse. It can make it more difficult for people to find common ground and engage in constructive dialogue, which is necessary for effective governance.

Civilized debate is necessary for a functioning democracy.

Mosaic's Tale

In vineyard's grasp, a secret slept,
Beneath the vines, where grapes wept.
A tale of ancient Rome did lie,
Unveiled beneath an azure sky.
The earth did tremble, roots were swayed,
And with each spade, the past displayed.

A mosaic's tale, a Roman villa's song,
Their beauty lost, forgotten long.
Intricate tiles of blues and reds,
Assembled by long-vanished hands,
Depicting scenes of love and life,
In times of splendor, joy, and strife.
Each piece of glass and shard of stone,
A story told, a vision sown.

In silent awe, we now revere,
The artists' craft from yesteryear.
Through tesserae, the stories told,
A testament to love of old.
In ancient Rome, where hearts did beat,
Where passions flared and heroes meet.
Bacchus' blessing, vines entwined,
In villa's halls, their lives enshrined.

The echoes of a bygone age,
Imprinted on this earthly stage.
Their laughter, whispers, sorrow, fears,
Transcending time, they reappear,
Through tesserae and colors bold,
We glimpse the lives of men of old.
So let us raise our glasses high,
And toast to those who've passed us by.
For in this villa's buried splendor,
A mosaic's tale, we shall remember.

Are there time travelers?

In Cambridge, long ago, one fateful eve,
A party planned, one hard to conceive.
The host, a man of brilliance and wit,
Stephen Hawking, his stage was lit.
An invitation for time to bend,
To future guests, a hand extend.

With champagne, Krug, and hors d'oeuvres,
An event to test both time and nerves.
In 2009, the stage was set,
A rendezvous we won't forget.
But the invite, a twist, he'd hold,
Till party's end, the tale untold.
The question posed, a daring dare,
If time could bend, then who'd be there?
If travelers came, the truth would show,
The secrets of time's ebb and flow.
The clock struck twelve, the candles gleamed,
Yet empty chairs, a room unteemed.
No travelers came from future's door,
No footsteps danced upon the floor.

Did Hawking's plan unfold as thought,
With proof that time could not be bought?
Or had they hid, in shadows cast,
A quiet nod to science's past?
Perhaps his genius, so profound,
The ripples of time, he could confound.
His party stands in memory's haze,
A testament to the human craze.

To seek the truth, to question time,
The wonders of the cosmos' rhyme.
Though empty stood that fateful room,
His legacy, forever to bloom.

Bacchus' Curse

Bacchus blessing, god of wine and vine,
Whose touch imbued with the divine,
You brought to us ecstatic glee,
Unleashing creativity.
In vineyards' grasp, your presence thrived,
As golden sun and rain contrived,
To grow the grapes upon the vine,
That turned to nectar most divine.
The Romans hailed your boundless might,
In frenzied states, day and night,
As Eleutherios, you set them free,
To dance and sing in revelry.
Your power, through wine, did course,
Through every man and woman's force,
A liberation from the chains,
That bound their hearts and dulled their brains.
In drunken stupor, minds would soar,
Unlocking thoughts ne'er known before,
Religious fervor, artistry,
Born of your touch, and ecstasy.
Oh Bacchus, god of wild abandon,
You taught us to embrace what we can,
The spontaneous and unrestrained,
The hidden beauty in the profane.
In life's embrace, you did imbue,
The freedom that the spirit knew,
To dance and laugh, to love and sing,
To seize the joy that life may bring.
Let us remember, in your name,
The fire that burns within the flame,
And celebrate, in endless praise,
The god of wine, who lights our days.

Truth and Lies

In the realm of truths and lies,
A subtle dance, a grand disguise.
For truth remains, unyielding, strong,
Though disbelieved, it carries on.
A lie may spread, like wildfire's might,
Its tendrils dark, embracing night.

And yet, a lie, it still remains,
No matter how its grip sustains.
The truth stands tall, a sentinel,
A bastion, proud and seminal.
Though voices wane, and doubt may rise,
It perseveres, unwavering, wise.
A lie, so crafty and beguiling,
Twists and turns, its victims smiling.
Embraced by all, a falsehood spread,
But still, a lie, when all is said.

The test of time, the truth withstands,
A steady rock, midst shifting sands.
It knows no bounds, no compromise,
A beacon bright, in darkened skies.
A lie may thrive, in shadows cast,
But fleeting, false, it cannot last.
For in the end, the truth prevails,
A shining light, when darkness sails.
Hold fast to truth, though lone it seems,
And let it guide you, like a dream.
For in its stead, a lie will fade,
As truth endures, and fears allayed.

We are the Stars

We are the stars, they are the stripes,
Together, bound, in dreams and plights.
A tapestry, a land so vast,
Yet fractured, torn, a shadow cast.
In unity, our strength resides,
A nation's heart, where hope abides.
To mend the rifts, to heal the wounds,
We must unite, or face our doom.
The drowning of the poor, we see,
A weight that drags on liberty.
The rich grow richer, day by day,
While dreams of many fade away.
A fairer land, we must conceive,
A place where all can hope, believe.
No more the chasms, nor divides,
One heart, one pulse, where love resides.
For every star, a voice, a light,
A chance to rise, to join the fight.
In every stripe, a story told,
A journey brave, a spirit bold.
Together, we can forge a path,
A way to heal, to quell the wrath.
With hands outstretched, a kind embrace,
We'll build a land of truth and grace.
No longer stars and stripes apart,
But interwoven, heart to heart.
For in this union, we shall find,
A brighter dawn, a world combined.

History and Reparations

While some argue that racism would cease with reparations paid,
It's crucial that we understand the wounds that still pervade.
Reparations may address the debt, the past injustices,
But healing takes more than amends, it needs a deeper consciousness.
In California, some deny the need for reparation,
Claiming slavery did not touch this part of the nation.
Yet history reveals the truth, the pain and exploitation,
Of Native peoples and the Japanese, a tainted foundation.
For Indian children were enslaved, in Los Angeles 'til 1920,
A legal practice, hidden well, a truth that's dark and weighty.
The gold rush brought a wave of crimes, on native lands encroaching,
Displacing them, disrupting lives, the culture nearly vanquishing.
And let us not forget the plight, of Japanese Americans,
Interned post-Pearl Harbor, caged, their dignity forsaken.
Incarcerated for their roots, suspicion cast upon them,
Their lives uprooted, dreams destroyed, a chapter dark and solemn.
Reparations can't erase, the scars that still remain,
The echoes of injustice, the memories of pain.
They may provide a starting point, a step toward restoration,
But healing lies in unity, and a true reconciliation.
To claim that racism will end, with reparations alone,
Ignores the truth, the work ahead, the seeds that have been sown.
For change must come from deep within, the hearts and minds of many,
A journey toward a better world, where justice flows aplenty.

Sources:

1. Madley, Benjamin. "California's Yuki Indians: Defining Genocide in Native American History." Western Historical Quarterly 39, no. 3 (2008): 303-332.
2. Los Angeles Star, "City and County Property Tax Assessment," September 7, 1861.

3. Daniels, Roger. "The Internment of Japanese Americans." OAH Magazine of History 17, no. 2 (2003): 12-17.

4. Saito, Natsu Taylor. "Justice Held Hostage: U.S. Disregard for International Human Rights When Inconsistent with Its Sense of Self-Interest." American Indian Law Review 29, no. 2 (2004/2005): 345-383.

Golden Chains Unraveled

In a land of golden dreams, a story oft untold,
Of native servitude, and greed that took its hold.
A source reveals the truth, the darkness at its core,
A chapter of injustice, in California's lore.
The gold rush lured the many, with promises of wealth,
But in its wake, it brought destruction, suffering, and stealth.
For native lives were torn apart, in chains, they were confined,
Their freedom and their dignity, abandoned and maligned.
The fields and mines exploited them, in search of gleaming ore,
The landscape changed, the rivers bled, the earth forevermore.
As settlers rushed, the native lives, were cast aside like chaff,
Their very existence threatened, in this brutal aftermath.
Their labor stolen, families split, their heritage erased,

In servitude, their dreams were crushed, a culture laid to waste.
Forced to toil in foreign lands, their spirits worn and weary,
The weight of chains upon their souls, a burden dark and dreary.
California is still the land of gold, the truth we must confront,
A history of servitude, a legacy old and new, that still haunts.
To honor those who've suffered, we must ensure they're heard,
Their stories told, their pain acknowledged, in every single word.
If we don't learn from history, the lessons it provides,
To seek the truth, embrace the past, and mend the great divides.
For only then can healing come, and justice be restored,
In a land where once the native peoples, free and proud, had soared.

Source:
Gold Chains: The Hidden History of Slavery in California (2021).
American Civil Liberties Union of Northern California. Retrieved
from https://www.aclunc.org/sites/goldchains/index.html

Narrow Minds

In The Valley, where shadows loom,
A reputation, darkly blooms,
Of minds so set in days of old,
Where narrow thoughts and hearts take hold.
A man proclaims with voice so sure,
That slavery's stained, his land's so pure,
No reparations need they pay,
For past misdeeds, not theirs, he'd say.
But history speaks of darker times,
Of Indian children, servitude's crime,
In Los Angeles, not long ago,
A century past, the truth we know.
The Japanese internment, too,
Incarceration, hearts turned blue,
The gold rush brought a tide of pain,
The scars of which, still long remain.
But dialogue, it seems, is lost,
In fiery words and hate, exhaust,
With insults thrown and minds so closed,
No empathy, just blame imposed.
"Put down the crack pipe," some would jeer,
"Be gone!" they shout, or "Disappear!"
"Go play in traffic," so unkind,
No space for truth or change of mind.

In conversations, rifts do grow,
When ignorance and pride bestow,
No chance for healing, growth, or grace,
Just blame and anger in their place.
Too closed-minded to strive to find a common ground,
To share our truths, let love resound,
For closed minds, with their heads in the sand,
No hope or plan to understand,
so please go follow your own command,
And go.

War and Bluster

In distant lands, where whispers blow,
A grand parade, a fearsome show.
Downtown streets they stride,
A painted march, with aims they hide.
The missiles gleam, the banners wave,
As soldiers march, their faces brave.
But deep within their hearts reside,
The thoughts and fears they must abide.
Do they ponder on the human toll,
The lives consumed, the hearts they stole?
Or is their gaze fixed solely on,
The pageantry, the threat they've drawn?
A game of power, a show of force,
A bravado fed by dark discourse.
Failing men, with desperate stakes,
Inflate their worth, as tension breaks.
A dance of war, of fragile pride,
The reason for the strife worldwide.
For in this grand display, we see,
The cost of blind supremacy.
And yet, within this somber scene,
A hope persists, a light unseen.
That reason, love, and peace may sway,
The hearts of those who march today.
For understanding is the key,
To break the chains of enmity.
And in our quest to heal the rift,
May we all seek a brighter shift.

Words are my Shield

In verse, we find a refuge fine,
A place where humor heals the mind.
With words, we paint a tapestry,
Of laughter amid pain's journey.
When life's burdens weigh us down,
And sorrows threaten us to drown,
Let poetry become our guide,
To find the humor that's inside.
For in each rhyme, a truth unveiled,
A chuckle where despair once dwelled,
We stitch our wounds with metered lines,
And find relief through humor's signs.
The limerick, the pun, the jest,
Remind us how life's but a test,
And as we navigate the strife,
Humor breathes new joy to life.
In stanzas we, our woes confide,
And pain's sharp edges gently hide.
For with each word that we compose,
A door to laughter we disclose.
Dance and scream with poetry,
And laugh at life's absurdity,
For in the end, we'll surely see,
Humor heals the heart in verse, so free.

Possessions

Possessions that I hold so dear,
You fill my heart with love and fear,
Bound to you, I cannot flee,
For you possess and captivate me.
You bring me comfort, joy, and cheer,
Surrounded by the things I've gathered near,
Yet deep within, a conflict brews,
This love and hate, forever fused.
I cherish every trinket, every tome,

Each object that I call my own,
But shackled by the weight you bear,
I gasp for breath in cluttered air.
These walls adorned with art and flair,
My haven, refuge from despair,
Yet, as I dwell in your embrace,
I yearn for freedom, open space.
For every item I acquire,
It feeds a never-ending fire,

Consuming, grasping, wanting more,
A constant battle I endure.
This dance of love and hate, we weave,
In tangled webs, we coexist and cleave,
Can I release this grip, I pray,
To find the balance, light the way?
With mindful care, I must discern,
Which treasures hold a place, a turn,
To let go of that which binds,
And seek the peace within my mind.
In this struggle, I must face,
The truth that lies behind the chase,
To learn that things, both great and small,
Cannot possess my heart, my all.

Woven Words

In woven words, a tapestry divine,
The art of poetry, a dance, a shrine.
With every line, a world unveiled,
A universe of thoughts regaled.
A painter's stroke, but not of brush,
In metaphors and rhymes we trust.
A canvas made of language, bold,
A story etched, a tale retold.
Each verse a thread, a vibrant hue,
To paint the scenes we thought we knew.
And yet, the deeper meanings gleam,
The hidden truths, the poet's dream.
A secret shared, a knowing glance,
In poems we find our minds' romance.
An inside joke, a mystery,
A glimpse beyond what eyes can see.
For poetry, a journey through,
The labyrinth of thoughts we brew.
A tapestry of dreams, desires,
A dance of words that never tires.
To delve, to seek, to understand,
The secrets penned by poet's hand.
A joyous journey through the maze,
Of life's reflections, thoughts ablaze.
In verse we find a solace rare,
A world of beauty, truth laid bare.
With every line, a passion's flight,
To paint the soul, and share the light.

Threads in a Tapestry

In the tapestry of life, threads intertwine,
The colors of us and them, both yours and mine.
We weave our connections, so close and tight,
Expecting them always to hold through the night.
We take for granted the love that we share,
Assuming our people will always be there.
Through thick and thin, our hearts interlace,
Yet sometimes we falter, the truth we must face.
For when the facade begins to crack,
And reality's weight bears down our back,
We come to see that what we believed,
Might not be so true, and we stand deceived.
The open heart and the honest word,
Can sometimes cut deeper than the sharpest sword.
And when we reveal our truest selves,
We may find our people locked in distant shells.
For these ties, so strong and so dear,
Can change in a moment, dissolve into fear.
And we're left to wonder, where did we go wrong?
As we pick up the pieces, try to stay strong.
But know that within, we can learn and grow,
In the face of coldness, we'll find a new glow.
For though the love may not be as we thought,
We'll find a new path, with wisdom hard-wrought.
Remembering moments, the love that was real,
Learn from the heartache, and slowly, we'll heal.
In the dance of life, we stumble and sway,
But the love we once knew will guide us, each day.

Primordial Brains

Inspired by a quote from Tristan Harris.

In ancient realms of instinct we reside,
With primal urges, deep within, we strive,
To navigate the shadows, swirling wide,
A sea of knowledge, where we dive and dive.

Midst feudal thoughts, our leaders forge their reign,
In towers tall, they sculpt our world with care,
But hearts of old do not the future tame,
They grasp at dreams, that once were only air.

God-like technology, now in our hands,
Commands the stars and whispers to the wind,
Awakes the dawn and paints the shifting sands,
Yet, in its grasp, we tremble and rescind.

Three realms entwined, a paradox we weave,
A dance of chaos, fears, and hopes marred,
As gods and beasts, our human hearts conceive,
A future where our fates and souls are charred.

In whispers faint, the echoes of our past,
The wisdom of the ancients calls our name,
To reconcile the powers we amass,
And walk the line 'tween progress and disdain.

Unite, the ancient and the new,
From primordial depths to cosmic heights,
To forge a world with visions bright and true,
Where wisdom reigns and human hearts take flight.

War of Words

In battles fierce, where iron strikes at bone,
And fields are strewn with lives and dreams undone,
There lies a path, more subtle, yet unknown,
To wage a war where hearts and minds are won.

A war of words, where tongues are weapons keen,
And thoughts, like arrows, pierce the veils of night,
They spark a fire, in shadows unforeseen,
And guide us to a place where truth ignites.

Let voices rise, like armies on the shore,
But not to drown the world in blood and tears,
Instead, to reach the hearts we once ignored,
To conquer fears and bridge the gap of years.

In understanding, may we find our grace,
As differences dissolve in tender light,
For every word can heal the deepest chace,
And mend the wounds that weapons never might.

So raise the flag of dialogue and peace,
Where every voice is valued and embraced,
Let empathy and patience never cease,
As through our words, the bonds of love are traced.

For in this war, the spoils are ours to gain,
A world where hearts are woven, thread by thread,
And in the tapestry of life, we'll stain,
The colors bright of unity, not dread.

The war of words, a bloodless battleground,
Where tongues are swords, and thoughts as arrows fly,
In reasoned discourse, common ground is found,
With open hearts, we see through others' eyes.

No shattered homes, no lives in disarray,
In conversations, progress finds its way,
We bridge divides, as night turns into day,
And paint a world where hope and peace hold sway.

Let arguments and dialogues commence,
In parliaments and homes where minds are met,
For through the art of speech, we make amends,
And forge a bond that time shall not forget.

So take your stand, with words as weapons wield,
And strive to mend the wounds that war has made,
For in this clash of thoughts, our fates are sealed,
By understanding's power, the world remade.

Forgiveness

In the chambers of a heart that bled,
A story weaves of loss unsaid,
A river of grief, its waters red,
A path where forgiveness refused to tread.

The sun once shone on love's embrace,
Now shadows creep, in darkness chase,
With fractured hearts and bitter taste,
The bonds of trust forever laced.

As autumn leaves fall to the ground,
In whirlwinds of despair, we're bound,
The hallowed song of hope resounds,
Yet forgiveness hides, remains unfound.

How can we soar on broken wings,
When shattered dreams in silence sing?
Embrace the pain that parting brings,
And seek the solace hope can cling.

In moonlit skies, the stars align,
A dance of light, a cosmic sign,
To navigate the stormy brine,
And sail towards a future, undefined.

In the quiet night, we learn to mend,
The tattered threads that fate has rent,
Weaving new patterns, strength to lend,
For life's next chapter to ascend.

Though forgiveness may elude our grasp,
The courage to move on, we clasp,
The will to heal, the strength to rasp,
A symphony of love, with no strings attached.

So let the winds of change take flight,
Carry us forth from darkest night,
Into the dawn's redeeming light,
Where hearts unite, and dreams reignite.

Embrace the Day

In shadows deep, where weary hearts reside,
A tale unfolds, of redemption's quest,
Yet oft we find, with truth we dare not bide,
And don the masks, which shroud our true behest.

A cycle spun, through lies we weave and wear,
In vain attempts to break the chains that bind,
Yet in this dance, we find we're unaware,
That falsehood's grip entwines our hearts and minds.

To free ourselves, we yearn for brighter days,
And whisper tales of hope, in twilight's hues,
But like a moth, entranced by flame's display,
We're lured to lies, as truth we dare not choose.

The cycle turns, a carousel of dreams,
Where on this ride, we're blind to our own fate,
Yet deep within, the ember's glow still gleams,
A spark of truth, that yearns to liberate.

In courage bold, we face the mirror's gaze,
And strip away the masks we've worn for years,
Embrace the truth, let go of false displays,
And through redemption's fire, our hearts are seared.

For in this trial, our true selves are unveiled,
The lies we've spun, like cobwebs, fall away,
And in the ashes, new paths are revealed,
A chance to break the cycle, and embrace the day.

Listen

In the realm of voices, a truth lies concealed,
A wisdom that's waiting to be revealed,
For when we give voice to our thoughts and our fears,
We echo the knowledge of yesteryears.

But within the silence, a secret unfolds,
A promise of insight, a tale yet untold,
For when we lend ear to the whispers of life,
We open our hearts to the world and its strife.

When we talk, we revisit the paths we have trod,
A chorus of memories, a familiar road,
A symphony of echoes, a well-traveled way,
Yet bound by the limits of what we can say.

But when we listen, the world comes alive,
In the hush of the moment, new wisdoms arrive,
A tapestry woven of myriad hues,
A canvas of learning, an opus of truths.

In the quiet surrender to the art of the ear,
We embrace the unknown, the far and the near,
For in every heartbeat, in each whispered word,
A story unfolds, a message is heard.

So let us seek silence, the stillness embrace,
To learn from each other, in this shared space,
For the gift of true listening, so humbly bestowed,
Is the key to the treasures that life has to show.

Catching Empathy

In a world of chaos, a whisper takes flight,
A call for empathy, to banish the night,
For empathy's the key, to unlock the chains,
Of climate, of poverty, the hurt that remains.

Too often our nets, they are cast far too small,
A family, a tribe, a faith to enthral,
But in casting them narrow, we fail to see,
The world beyond borders, where all can be free.

If we learn from the Kiwis, their spirit of one,
Five million strong, united, undone,
A world of inclusion, where all find a place,
In the net of compassion, we'll all find embrace.

For empathy's power, it reaches beyond,
The limits of kinship, the ties that we bond,
When we see "us" as all, in the grandest of scales,
The barriers crumble, as unity prevails.

Through empathy's lens, we can face the unknown,
Climate change conquered, as seeds of hope are sown,
With hearts intertwined, poverty shall wane,
A world built on kindness, where all feel the gain.

And in civil rights battles, we'll march side by side,
For the rights of each other, our hearts open wide,
United in purpose, a vision we share,
Of a future where all can thrive, free from despair.

If we cast wide the net of our care,
To embrace every soul, every burden we bear,
For empathy's the key, to healing the strife,
And creating a world where all can find life.

Unsung

In the tapestry of life, a quiet thread is sewn,
By those who toil in silence, their faces yet unknown,
Their achievements often whispered, their purpose strong and true,
They weave a world of wonder, in shades of every hue.

These unsung heroes labor, in shadows and in light,
Their focus, laser-guided, their vision shining bright,
No need for self-promotion, for fame, or for applause,
Their dedication steadfast, a humble, noble cause.

We owe our deepest gratitude, to those who pave the way,
Who shape the world around us, in every act and play,
Their impact often subtle, but felt in countless ways,
A debt of thanks unspoken, our silent praise we raise.

In the quiet of their journey, they seek no grand acclaim,
No trophies or ovations, no spotlight to their name,
Yet in their anonymity, a power we discern,
The strength of perseverance, a lesson we must learn.

For those who work in silence, their hearts a compass true,
They guide us through the darkness, a beacon cutting through,
Their selfless acts of kindness, a testament to grace,
A world transformed by actions, that time will not erase.

So let us honor those unseen, who strive without fanfare,
Whose impact resonates within, a world beyond compare,
For in their quiet purpose, a truth we must embrace,
Gratitude unasked for, is gratitude most deserved in place.

Epilogue

In the Garden of Political Poetry

As we reach the closing pages of "Political Poetry," we are reminded of the transformative power that words, rhythm, and imagery can have on our understanding of the world around us. Christina's masterful pen has crafted a tapestry of poems that delicately express the intricacies of modern politics and the need for policies that work for everyone. By illustrating that everything is local when it comes to people and their experiences, she invites us to see ourselves not just as individuals, but as part of a wider, interwoven tapestry.

Throughout this collection, Christina has shown us that even in the vast, complex world of politics, the truest way to make a difference is by nurturing connections to the people around us and the natural world that sustains us. The nature-based poetry woven through the book serves as a reminder that we are all connected, and that this connection is as essential as it is beautiful.

In the fleeting, magical moments that Christina captures in her writing, we are drawn to the realization that life is indeed short. She inspires us to embrace these moments, to live life fully, and to be mindful of the impact our choices have on both our local communities and the broader world. Her words evoke a sense of responsibility, encouraging us to become agents of change in our own lives, as well as catalysts for a more equitable and just society.

"Political Poetry" is a celebration of the human spirit, resilience, and our shared humanity. It highlights the importance of empathy and understanding, urging us to listen to one another's stories and to appreciate the beauty in our differences. Christina's poetry teaches us that the key to finding common ground lies in recognizing our shared connection to the natural world and the inherent value of every life within it.

As we close the book and absorb the messages within, let us carry the essence of "Political Poetry" with us in our daily lives. May we be reminded of the power we have to shape the world, to create a more compassionate society, and to work together toward a future that is fair and inclusive for all.

And as we walk through the garden of political poetry, let us pause to smell the flowers, admire the beauty around us, and remember that the world we create is ultimately a reflection of our hearts and minds. Together, let us write the next chapter in the story of our shared journey, a chapter filled with love, understanding, and the magic of connection.

About the Author

Christina Walsh is an internationally published artist, and environmental sustainability professional. Christina's work is a reflection of her passion for justice, equality, and environmental sustainability. As an artist, Christina has exhibited her work in galleries in the United States, Europe. Her art, as an acrylic painter is characterized by portraits and abstract ideas incorporating emotion and nature and the exploration of the relationships between humans and the natural world. Through her work, Christina seeks to inspire others to think critically about the world around us and to take action to create a more just and sustainable future. She is a dedicated environmental activist and works to promote sustainability in her personal and professional life. Christina's passion for art, writing, and environmental sustainability shines through in everything she does. Her work is a powerful call to action and a reminder of the beauty and value of the natural world.

Printed in the United States
by Baker & Taylor Publisher Services